ENGINEERING

A Primer

Jeffrey B. Connor, P.E.

Copyright © 2018 by Jeffrey B. Connor, P.E.

All rights reserved. This book or any portion thereof may not be reproduced or used in any manner whatsoever without the express written permission of the publisher except for the use of brief quotations in a book review.

My fascination with water began at eight years of age.
Walking home from school in the rain, I remember squatting
by the curb watching water flow to the drain.
I have not stopped watching water flow.

JEFFREY CONNOR, P.E.

Contents

Introduction

Science can amuse and fascinate us all, but it is engineering that changes the world.

Isaac Asimov

This is the book I wish I'd had before starting my engineering education. This book contains concepts that are elementary for any engineer—concepts that lay a firm foundation for those beginning their education.

The structure of this book takes the reader from the language of engineering to concepts of design. This is not a textbook. Rather, it is an overview of critical ideas used within the profession. Its method is simple, explaining concepts and giving illustrative examples. The only background the reader needs is an interest in engineering and knowledge of algebra and trigonometry.

Chapter 1, LANGUAGE, is an introduction to technical communication. Many readers will find some of the material to be a review, such as geometry and numbers. Others may find sections such as calculus and probability the first introduction to a topic. This language is the basis of how engineers think and communicate.

Chapter 2, RELATIONSHIPS, illustrates an intermediate step in design. These equations, called relationships, quantify the effect of an action. Examples start with data and then determine a mathematical relationship where that function best predicts the effect of an action. In most cases, these "if this, then that" relationships are correlations and often useful in prediction. The more valuable and less common relationships determine cause and effect. Most relationships are partially causal, but teasing out the causal part is difficult.

Chapter 3, DESIGN, starts with ideas of opportunity cost and marginal design. These two topics illustrate the fact that a good design is a design that is "good enough." There are no ideal or perfect designs; all are, for good reason, compromises of conflicting criteria and constraints. Furthermore, cost is always a defining constraint. The "First Principles" section in this chapter introduces and illustrates the use of forces and moments (torque), the basic tools used when designing physical objects. The chapter then introduces two common first principles: Archimedes' principle—the principle itself is only a single sentence that was written over 2,000 years ago. Archimedes' insight has remained unchanged to the present day, and its usefulness is undiminished. The chapter ends with a final principle, Bernoulli's, selected to demonstrate the power of its—and other first principles'—universality. You'll find several worked examples of these topics.

After high school, beginning engineering students will continue to take classes such as calculus, statics, and statistics without gaining a feel for their interdependency, especially when used in engineering design. As an example, I had very little appreciation for the usefulness and pervasiveness of probability until my senior year in college, and I only fully understood its importance when I went to graduate school. I then used it daily as a practicing engineer.

Some have described engineering education as creating an inventory of useful problem-solving tools. Often, an engineer will solve a problem by using these tools in situations that are different than the context in which they were taught.

Every practicing engineer's toolbox will be different, and many engineers may not realize the potential of their tools. Before and during my education, I worked in both land surveying and navigation at sea. While instruments and techniques differed, land surveying and navigation have the same purpose: determining the location of a position on earth. While the equipment and methods were different in the two environments, the principles were the same. It's this universality of principles that makes them so valuable. After graduation, I practiced as a hydraulic engineer, working with water flow and storage in a variety of environments. By necessity, I had to broaden my knowledge and increase the number and variety of my tools.

The four first principles discussed in chapter 3 are only a small fraction of countless others. As you gain experience in engineering, you will have a set of favorites, but remember that there are many others that, if understood, could be used in new ways for new designs. This broadening of knowledge changes your perception of the world. For instance, after a statics course, you will view a bridge with a new eye, and after studying probability, you will be more explicitly conscious of its usefulness in making both professional and personal decisions. These are examples of the concept of thinking like an engineer.

As a last point, it is worth remembering that our understanding of natural phenomena is small. No model is ever true—for two basic reasons. First, we are continuously discovering more truths. Second, the world is too complicated. The best we can do is to create models that are useful.

Basically, there are three models that predict natural phenomena: quantum mechanics, Newtonian physics, and relativity. Most engineers understand and see the world through the lens of gravity-based Newtonian physics. The other models of the world are equally valid but less understood.

In the smaller-scaled world of atoms and sub-atomic particles, quantum mechanics is used to predict the interaction between tiny particles that do not conform to the physics of the visible world. Newtonian-based models with deterministic predictions do not work on this size scale.

On the large scale of space and the universe, Newtonian models again fail to predict. Einstein's theories of general and special relativity conflict with the foundational aspects of Newton's laws. With Einstein's theories, time and mass are not constant, the effects noted by different observers are a function of the observers' relative motion, and gravity is a wave.

These more recent models are foreign and nonsensical to most of us, but they are nonetheless true. Without understanding and modeling the variable passage of time, global positioning systems would not be possible. The probabilistic outcomes in quantum mechanics do not meet any definition of common sense, yet quantum computers exist, are useful, and hold great promise.

Conflicting models are presented because of the need to know what you don't know. Acknowledging ignorance can be humbling, yet it often leads to seeking new knowledge that may be able to solve previously unsolvable problems or to improve current solutions.

I envy the new student of engineering. Knowledge, ingenuity, and computing power are advancing rapidly, and the opportunities to apply new knowledge and tools to improve the human condition are endless.

1

Language

W. E. B. Dubois

Engineering solves problems: not esoteric, theoretical, or merely interesting problems, but problems that are very much in the real world. To solve these problems requires a fundamental understanding of the language that is used to describe and understand the nature of the world in which we work. Much like other spoken and written languages, it starts with the basic building blocks of numbers and units that are manipulated and arranged to give both understanding and insight.

1.1 Numbers

Like any discipline, science, engineering, and the technical arts observe and describe the world using a language that is essential in communicating and understanding natural phenomena. Much like the alphabet in writing, numbers are the foundation of this understanding.

Numbers can be defined in a variety of ways, and we will use the four types detailed in Table 1.

Table 1. Common Number Types

Type	Number of Digits	Notes
Measurement	Finite	Never exact.
Count	Infinite	Always exact (e.g., number of people), whole number.
Conversion	Finite or Infinite	As a count, a conversion is exact (e.g., 12 inches in a foot). Other conversions are not exact. For example, 57.2958 degrees equals one radian.
Transcendental	Essentially Infinite	π, e.

A common error when working with numbers is displaying an inappropriate number of digits. In both engineering and everyday life, we essentially live in a three or four-digit world. For example, a house may be advertised for sale at $253,000, which has three significant digits, or perhaps $252,900, which has four significant digits, although arguably, the four-digit price reflects marketing more than reality. Likewise, in engineering, we commonly understand and predict natural phenomena to only three or four digits. Showing excessive digits in a solution is evidence of a fundamental misunderstanding of your calculations.

Numbers are described in terms of accuracy and precision. An accurate number is one that is close to the "true" value. A precise number is one that is measured to a small increment, usually expressed by a large number of digits. If there has been no mistake in counting, a count is always perfectly accurate and infinitely precise, that is, the number has an infinite number of significant digits. For example, a count of three objects is the number three with an infinite number of zeros after the decimal point (3.000000...). Transcendental numbers are assumed—and for all practical purposes are—infinitely precise. Measurements, however, are always imprecise to some degree. As is explained in more detail below, there is no "true" value of a measurement against which to compare for accuracy, and a measurement's precision can always be increased. The number of significant digits is a way to display precision—generally, the more precise the number, the more significant digits are displayed.

The rules for determining the appropriate number of digits can become a bit complex, but in general:

When multiplying or dividing, the answer is presented with the same precision as the number with the fewest significant digits. When adding or subtracting, the precision of the answer is to the same precision as the least precise individual number.

Example 1.

Multiplying or dividing measurements

$$(1.35)(1.2) = 1.62$$

However, the answer is 1.6, because a three-digit value (1.35) multiplied by a two-digit value (1.2) solution in a two-digit result (1.6).

Example 2.

Adding or subtracting measurements

$$23.137 + 130.2 = 153.337$$

However, the answer is 153.3 because a value with a precision of three decimal places (23.137) added to a value with one decimal place precision (130.2) results in an answer of one-decimal precision (153.3).

Example 3.

Multiplying or dividing a count and a measurement.
If three objects together weigh 17.2 lbf, their average weight is:

$$\frac{17.2\,\text{lbf}}{3\,\text{objects}} = \frac{5.73\,\text{lbf}}{\text{object}}$$

In this case, the number of objects is a count with an infinite number of digits. Therefore, the result (5.73 lbf per object) is three digits because the number with the fewest digits (17.2) determines the number of digits in the answer.

> **Example 4.**
>
> Adding or subtracting counts
> There are 2 people in one room and 175 in another. There are a total of 177 people.

> **Example 5.**
>
> Multiplying or dividing counts
> There are 13 objects that are to be placed in boxes where each box has the capacity to hold 4 objects. The number of boxes required is calculated as:
>
> $$\frac{13 \text{ objects}}{4\dfrac{\text{objects}}{\text{box}}} = 3.25 \text{ boxes}$$
>
> A partial box does not make physical sense, so the solution must be rounded up to the next whole number: 4 boxes.

1.2 Units

Most numbers are associated with units, and analyzing units is a fundamental task of any engineer because units describe the nature and meaning of the numbers. A basic example is that an object travels 32 m in 2.0 s, resulting in a velocity of 16 m/s. If the object continues at the same velocity for an additional 3.0 s, it will have traveled an additional 48 m, because when multiplying 16 m/s by 3.0 s, seconds is in the denominator in the first value and in the numerator in the second value. They therefore cancel each other out and leave only meters.

Our language of physical phenomena is comprised of seven fundamental units: mass, length, time, light intensity, electric current, amount of a substance, and temperature. We will discuss only the first three: mass [M], length [L], and time [T], and we will use the square bracket and upper-case letter notation. From these fundamental units, often called base units, we can further derive other units. For instance, the derived unit of velocity is length over time, or $[L][T]^{-1}$.

Note the exponential notation where a negative indicates that the unit is in the denominator. As another example, force is equal to mass times acceleration: force $= [M][L][T]^{-2}$, where $[L][T]^{-2}$ is acceleration. Because force is so often used, it can be considered an honorary fundamental unit and is often denoted as [F].

The two predominant systems of units are the SI (international system, or metric) and the Imperial (English, US) system, see Table 2. Some engineers will work an entire career using one system almost exclusively, while others will use a combination in their work. The student of engineering must be comfortable using both.

Table 2. Units of Fundamental Measurement by System

System	Mass	Length	Time	Force	Gravitational Acceleration (g)
SI	Kilogram (kg)	Meter (m)	Second (s)	Newton (N)	9.81 m/s^2
Imperial	Slug	Foot (ft)	Second (s)	Pound-force (lbf)	32.2 ft/s^2

$F = ma$ is the definition of force. Weight is a particular type of force where $W = mg$. g is the acceleration due to gravity.

Mass in the Imperial system is confusing because two units are commonly used. Often used is pound-mass (lbm). A slug is the more correct unit because when using $F = ma$, the mass used must be a slug. A pound-mass is used for convenience and is simply numerically equal to a pound force. As an example, if an

Table 3. Examples of Derived Units

Unit	Fundamental Units	SI	Imperial
Force	$[M][L][T]^{-2}$	Newton (N)	pound-force (lbf)
Area	$[L]^2$	square meters (m^2)	ft^2
Velocity	$[L][T]^{-1}$	meters per second (m/s)	feet per second (ft/s)
Acceleration	$[L][T]^{-2}$	feet per second squared (ft/s^2)	meters per second squared (m/s^2)
Volume	$[L]^3$	liter (L)	gallon (gal)
Pressure	$[F][L]^{-2}$	Pascal (Pa)	pounds per square inch (psi)
Density	$[M][L]^{-3}$	kg/m^3 (ρ)	lbm/ft^3 (ρ)
Specific weight	$[F][L]^{-3}$	N/m^3 (γ)	lbf/ft^3 (γ)
Flow rate	$[L]^3[T]^{-1}$	cubic meters per second (Q)	gallons per minute (gpm), (Q)
Energy, Work, Heat	$[F][L]$	Joule (J), kilowatt-hour (kWh)	British thermal unit (Btu), kilowatt-hour (kWh)
Power	$[F][L][T]^{-1}$	kilowatt (kW)	kilowatt (kW), Horsepower (hp)

object weighs 214 lbf, its mass is $\dfrac{214\,\text{lbf}}{32.2\dfrac{\text{ft}}{\text{s}^2}} = 6.65$ slugs. Its mass can also be said to be 214 lbm. It is critical to know what mass units are being used. Confusing them leads to a result that is incorrect by a factor of 32.2. The loss of the Mars Climate Orbiter in 1999 is a well-known failure caused by the incorrect use of units. Always be explicit if a pound is mass or force; the notation lbf or lbm should be used.

Example 1.

To convert units of a value from one set of units to another, you must first confirm that the fundamental dimensions of the original unit are the same as the ending unit. As an example, in water supply, two common measures of flow rate are $\dfrac{\text{acre-ft}}{\text{day}}$ and $\dfrac{\text{m}^3}{\text{s}}$. To convert from one to the other, you need to know or look up: 24 hours $= 1$ day, $3{,}600$ s $= 1$ hour, 1 foot $= 0.3048$ m, and $43{,}560$ ft^2 $= 1$ acre. With this example of flow rate, the starting and ending units are both $[\text{L}]^3[\text{T}]$. Next, arrange the numerators and denominators such that the units cancel, and multiply as shown below.

To convert $56\,\dfrac{\text{acre-ft}}{\text{day}}$ to $\dfrac{\text{m}^3}{\text{s}}$:

$$\left(\frac{56.0\,\text{acre-ft}}{\text{day}}\right)\left(\frac{1\,\text{day}}{24\,\text{hr}}\right)\left(\frac{1\,\text{hr}}{3600\,\text{s}}\right)\left(\frac{43560\,\text{ft}^2}{1\,\text{acre}}\right)\cdot$$

$$\cdot\left(\frac{0.3048\,\text{m}}{1\,\text{ft}}\right)\left(\frac{0.3048\,\text{m}}{1\,\text{ft}}\right)\left(\frac{0.3048\,\text{m}}{1\,\text{ft}}\right)=\frac{0.800\,\text{m}^3}{\text{s}}$$

Example 2.

Units are also useful in understanding the nature of physical phenomena. As an example, power from a dam is created by using the potential energy of stored water and releasing it through a turbine located at a lower elevation. This converts potential energy to kinetic energy, which is used to generate electricity.

The power produced by a turbine is a function of the product of four units, the flowrate of water through the turbine (Q), the density of the water (ρ), the difference in elevation between the reservoir and the turbine (head, H), and a fourth unit. Find the missing unit. Refer to the table of units, Table 3, above.

From table: Power $= [\text{F}][\text{L}][\text{T}]^{-1}$

From table: Power $= [\text{M}][\text{L}][\text{T}]^{-2}\,[\text{L}]\,[\text{T}]^{-1}$

From given: Power $= (Q)(\rho)(H)$ (missing)

From given: Power $= [L]^3[T]^{-1} [M][L]^{-3} [L]$ [missing]

Power $= [M][L][T]^{-2} [L] [T]^{-1} = [L]^3[T]^{-1} [M][L]^{-3} [L]$ [missing]

[missing] $= [L][T]^{-2} =$ acceleration. In this case, acceleration due to gravity.

1.3 Mathematics

1.3.1 Geometry and Trigonometry

Much like knowing the alphabet and the times tables to a degree that the knowledge is ingrained, so should you know basic geometry and trigonometry. A few examples that you should know are below.

Right Angle Trigonometry

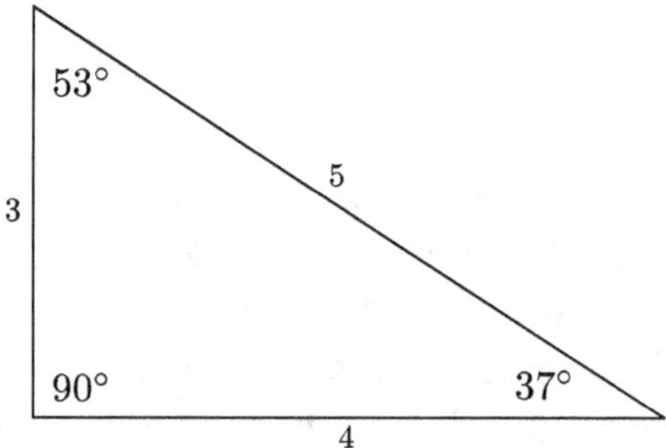

Figure 1. Right Triangle

Use Figure 1, showing the "3, 4, 5 triangle," to remind yourself of the basic calculations. Knowing any two of the values given, all other values can be calculated. The well-known 3, 4, 5 triangle is used as an example, but these relationships are valid for any right triangle. As a reminder, sin, cos, and tan are sine, cosine, and tangent, respectively. Also, a trig function with the raised to a power of -1 notation indicates the inverse of the value. This is also called the "arc" of an angle. Practice and be able to readily use these relationships.

Relationships and Examples

Table 4. Right Angle Relationships

Relationships
$A^2 + B^2 = C^2$
Sin = Opposite/Hypotenuse
Cos = Adjacent/Hypotenuse
Tan = Opposite/Adjacent

Table 5. Right Angle Examples

Examples
$3^2 + 4^2 = 5^2$
$3 = (5)(\mathrm{Sin}\,37°)$
$4 = (5)(\mathrm{Cos}\,37°)$
$4 = (5^2 - 3^2)^{1/2}$

1.3.2 Areas and Volumes

Obviously, you will have memorized many other useful formulas and relationships, but those shown can solve many problems when the problem is approached with the simplest method of solution in mind. See the two examples below.

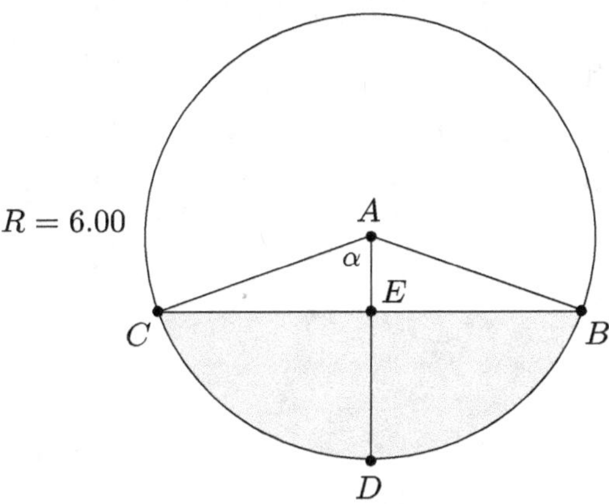

Figure 2. Flow Area in a Pipe

Example 1.

A 12.0 in diameter water pipe flows at a depth of 4.00 in as shown in Figure 2.
Calculate the area of the flow.

1. $ED = 4.00$ in; therefore, $AE = 2.00$ in

2. $\alpha = \cos^{-1}(2/6) = 70.5°$

3. Angle $CAB = (2)(\alpha) = 141°$

4. Area of $ACDBA$ $(141°/360°)(\pi)(6.00 \text{ in})^2 = 44.3 \text{ in}^2$

5. $CE = \sin(70.5°)(6.00 \text{ in}) = 5.65$ in

6. Area $CABEC = (2)(0.5)(5.65 \text{ in})(2.00 \text{ in}) = 11.3 \text{ in}^2$

7. Area water $= 44.3 \text{ in}^2 - 11.3 \text{ in}^2 = 33.0 \text{ in}^2$

If the volumetric flow rate is 0.650 ft³/s, find the velocity of the water flow.

1. $(33.0 \text{ in}^2)\left(\dfrac{1 \text{ ft}}{12 \text{ in}}\right)\left(\dfrac{1 \text{ ft}}{12 \text{ in}}\right) = (0.229 \text{ ft}^2)$

2. $\dfrac{0.650 \dfrac{\text{ft}^3}{\text{s}}}{0.229 \text{ ft}^2} = 2.84 \dfrac{\text{ft}}{\text{s}}$

Example 2.

Approximate the value of π by inscribing multi-sided geometry within a circle having a radius of 2.00. First, calculate the perimeter of a square. The circumference of the circle is $(2)(2.00)(\pi) = 12.5664$. I am showing more significant digits than justified to demonstrate that increasing the number of sides results in a more precise estimate of π.

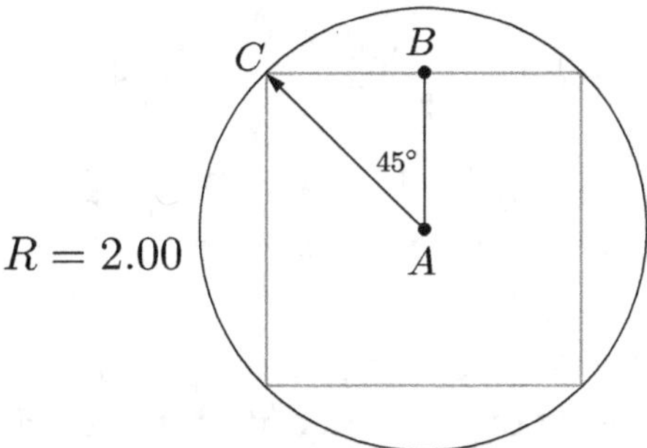

Figure 3. Square Inscribed within a Circle

Using Figure 3:

1. $CB = \sin(45°)(2.00) = 1.4142$

2. Total perimeter $= (8)(1.4142) = 11.3136$

Next, calculate the perimeter of a pentagon inscribed in a circle with a radius of 2.00.

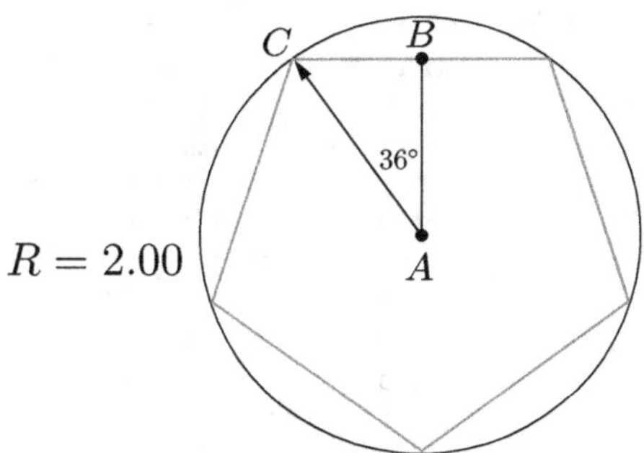

Figure 4. Pentagon Inscribed within a Circle

Referring to Figure 4:

1. $CB = \sin(36°)(2.00) = 1.1756$

2. Total perimeter $= (10)(1.41) = 11.7557$

It can be seen that the equation for the perimeter of a multi-sided object inscribed within a circle is:

$$\text{Perimeter} = \sin\left(\frac{180°}{N}\right)(N)(D) \qquad (1.1)$$

Where N is the number of sides and D is the diameter of the circle in which the polygon is inscribed.

Both Table 6 and Figure 5 demonstrate that as the number of sides of a regular polygon inscribed within a circle increases, the perimeter of that polygon approaches the circumference of the circle. The perimeter of an infinitely sided polygon would equal the circumference of the circle.

Table 6. Pi and the Number of Sides of an Inscribed Polygon

# of Sides	Diameter	Circumference	Perimeter	Ratio of Perimeter to π
4	4.00	12.566	11.314	0.9003
5	4.00	12.566	11.756	0.9355
6	4.00	12.566	12.000	0.9549
7	4.00	12.566	12.149	0.9668
8	4.00	12.566	12.246	0.9745
9	4.00	12.566	12.313	0.9798
10	4.00	12.566	12.361	0.9836

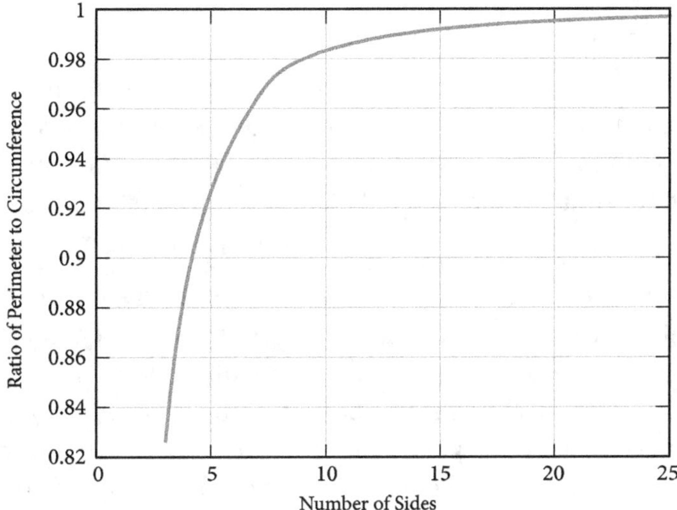

Figure 5. Ratio of Polygon Perimeters to Circumference

Looking at it another way, the value of pi can be approximated using the perimeter of a polygon where the value of "π" is calculated as perimeter/diameter. Table 7 shows that as the number of sides of a polygon increases, the calculated value of π approaches its true value.

Table 7. Estimating pi with Increasingly Sided Polygons

Sides	Diameter	Perimeter	"π"
4	4.00	11.3137	2.8284
5	4.00	11.7557	2.9389
6	4.00	12.0000	3.0000
7	4.00	12.1487	3.0372
8	4.00	12.2459	3.0615
9	4.00	12.3127	3.0782
10	4.00	12.3607	3.0902
11	4.00	12.3962	3.0991
12	4.00	12.4233	3.1058
13	4.00	12.4444	3.1111
14	4.00	12.4612	3.1153
15	4.00	12.4747	3.1187

1.3.3 Calculus

Calculus is commonly used throughout engineering and science and is essential in the solution of various problems. About 300 years ago, Sir Isaac Newton and Gottfried Leibniz simultaneously—and independently—developed modern calculus. The essence of calculus is the concept of infinitesimally small differences.

In mathematics, we manipulate numbers to create other numbers. Relationships are described by functions, and calculus uses functions to develop new functions. Calculus is either differential, where the rate of change (slope) of a function at any point is determined, or it is integral, where the area beneath a portion of a curve is determined. The examples shown here are quite simple and are meant to show the utility of calculus. Addressing the mechanics of calculus is beyond the scope of this book. Integrating and differentiating functions can often be quite difficult, requiring sophisticated methods to solve.

Integration and differentiation are related. For example, the integral of $y = 4x^2 - 2x + 5$ is written as $\int 4x^2 - 2x + 5 \, dx$, and the solution is $y = \frac{4}{3}x^3 - x^2 + 5x + \text{constant}$. You can see that the integral of a function increases the exponent of each term by one and divides the coefficient of that term by its new exponent. The derivative of the new function would be written as $\frac{dy}{dx}\left(\frac{4}{3}x^3 - x^2 + 5x\right)$, and it equals the original function $y = 4x^2 - 2x + 5$. The exponent of each term is decreased by one, and the coefficient of each term is multiplied by the exponent. The solution of an integral adds the constant C because the solution represents a family of solutions where the bounds can chage. The C acknowledges the possible use of various bounds.

Integration

As an example of integration, see Figure 6, which shows the relationship between time and the velocity of an object.

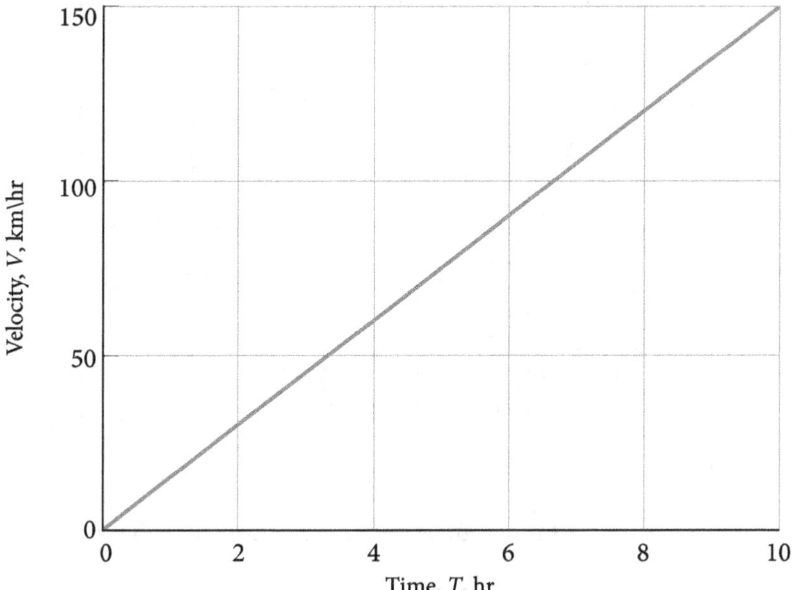

Figure 6. Velocity and Time

The function is $V = 15T$ where the object's velocity increases at a rate of 15 km every hour. The total distance traveled can be determined by finding the area under the curve. The area of a triangle is one half base times height, so in this case:

$$\text{Area} = \frac{1}{2}(T)(V) = \frac{1}{2}(10 \text{ hr})\left(150\frac{\text{km}}{\text{hr}}\right) = 750 \text{ km}$$

The "area under the curve" is conceptually different from "area" in geometry, which is stated in square units. In this example, the area under the curve gives us the distance we're looking for—a linear term because velocity times time equals distance.

With less precision, we could measure the area under the curve by calculating the sum of the areas of rectangles beneath the curve. For instance, a rectangle with a base length (ΔT, "Delta T") from 0 hr to 2 hr and a height of 30 km/hr has an area of 60 km. Likewise, the areas of the other rectangles are similarly calculated. When added together, the total area of the rectangles is 900 km. See Figure 7 and Table 8.

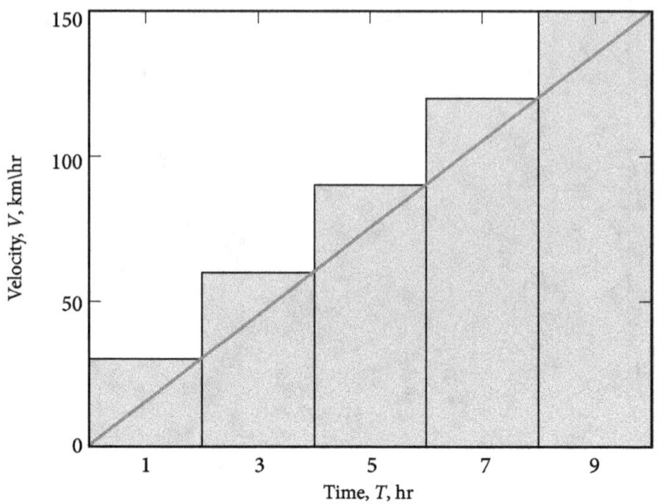

Figure 7. Rectangles at $\Delta T = 2.0$ hr, Area $= 900$ km

Table 8. Area of Rectangles at $\Delta T = 2.0$ hr

Time (hr)	0.0–2.0	2.0–4.0	4.0–6.0	6.0–8.0	8.0–10.0	Sum
Distance (km)	60	120	180	240	300	900

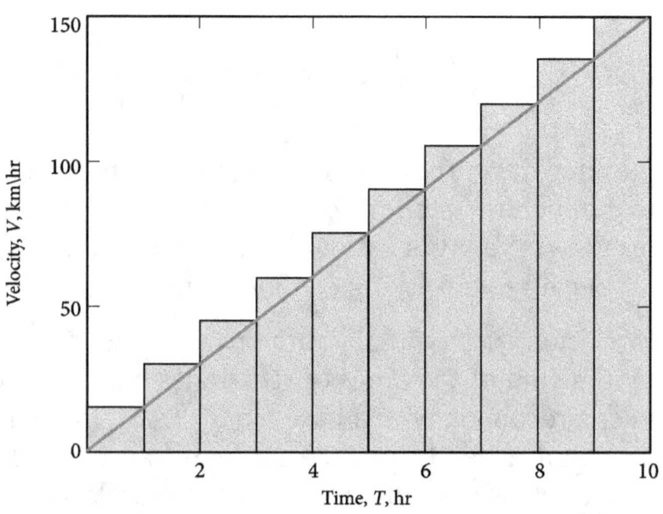

Figure 8. Rectangles at $\Delta T = 1.0$ hr, Area $= 825$ km

To more accurately find the area under the curve, ΔT could be lessened to one hour (see Figure 8). The sum of the rectangles equals 15 km + 30 km + 45 km + 60 km + 75 km + 90 km + 105 km + 120 km + 135 km + 150 km = 825 km.

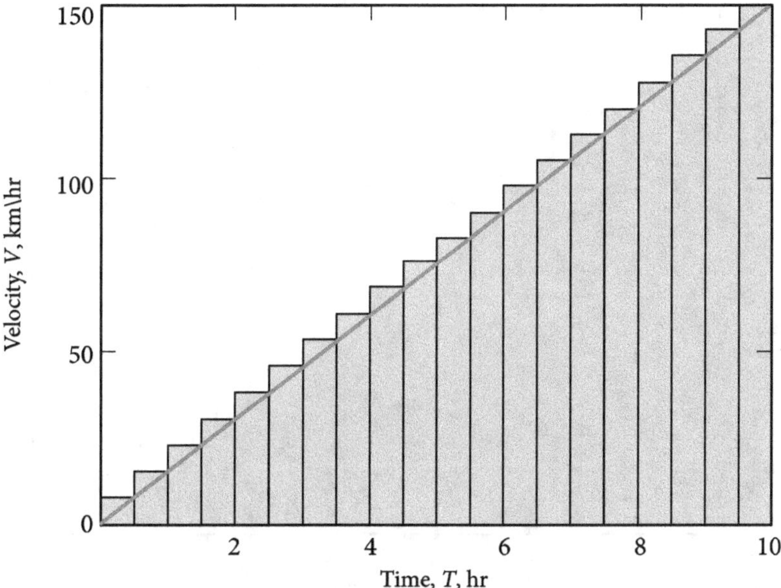

Figure 9. Rectangles at $\Delta T = 0.50$ hr, Area $= 788$ km

Closer still is using a base of $\Delta T = 0.5$ hr as shown in Figure 9. The sum of the rectangles equals 787.5 km. As ΔT becomes smaller, the area is more accurate and approaches the true value of 750 km.

Using an infinitesimally small ΔT results in *the* area.

We can also find the area under a curve with integral calculus. The integral of $V = 15T$ between $T = 0$ hr to $T = 10$ hr is written this way: $\int_0^{10} 15T \, dt$. Zero and 10 are the start and stop points of the integration as these are the bounds of the time we are interested in. In this integral, "dt" represents the ΔT we discussed previously, where the ΔT is infinitely small, which is the base of a rectangle whose height is measured to the line of the function.

Example 3.

Figure 10 shows the power consumption (kilowatts) of a commercial building over a period of five hours. The curve's equation is $P = T^3 - 6T^2 + 4T + 20$.

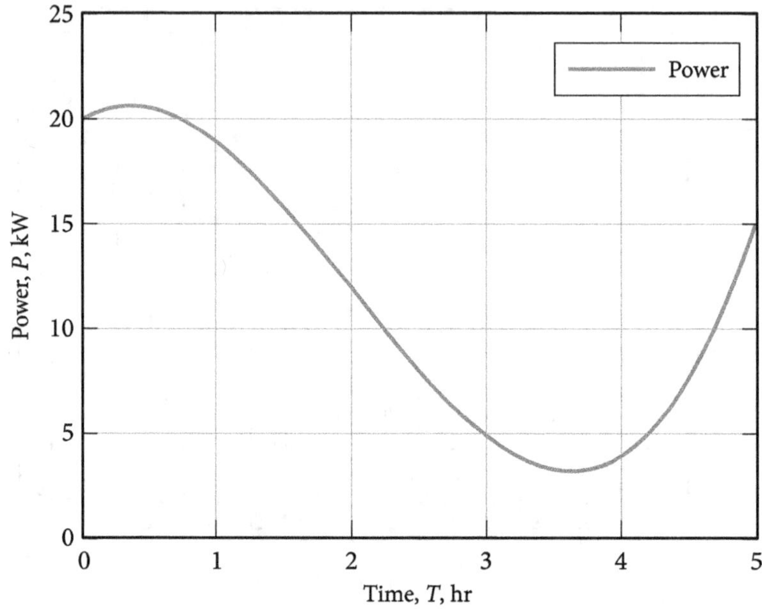

Figure 10. Power Demand over Time

To determine the total energy used over the period, integrate the equation from $T = 0$ hr to $T = 5$ hr.

$$\int_0^5 T^3 - 6T^2 + 4T + 20\, dT = \frac{T^4}{4} - 2T^3 + 2T^2 + 20T + \text{constant} \Big|_0^5$$

To find the area under the curve over a desired range, evaluate the integral with the upper limit (5) and then subtract the value of the integral at the lower limit (0). Assume that the constant equals zero. Recall that power times time equals energy.

The value of the integral at the upper range is

$$\text{At } T = 5: \quad \text{Energy} = \frac{5^4}{4} - 2(5^3) + 2(5^2) + 20(5)$$

$$= 156 - 250 + 50 + 100 = 56 \text{ kWh}$$

$$\text{At } T = 0: \quad \text{Energy} = 0 \text{ kWh}$$

Therefore, the energy used over the five-hour period is $56 \text{ kWh} - 0 \text{ kWh} = 56 \text{ kWh}$.

If we wanted to know the energy used between hours 1 and 4, we would evaluate the same integral over that time period.

$$\int_1^4 T^3 - 6T^2 + 4T + 20 \ dT$$

$$= \frac{T^4}{4} - 2T^3 + 2T^2 + 20T + \text{constant} \ \Big|_1^4$$

At $T = 4$:

$$\text{Energy} = \frac{4^4}{4} - 2(4^3) + 2(4^2) + 20(4)$$

$$= 64.0 - 128 + 32.0 + 80.0 = 48.0 \text{ kWh}$$

At $T = 1$,

$$\text{Energy} = \frac{1^4}{4} - 2(1^3) + 2(1^2) + 20(1)$$

$$= 0.25 - 2.00 + 2.00 + 20.0 = 20.3 \text{ kWh}$$

Therefore, the energy used from the first hour to the fourth hour is $48.0 \text{ kWh} - 20.3 \text{ kWh} = 27.7 \text{ kWh}$.

Differentiation

The derivative of a function determines the slope of a line tangent to the function at any point.

Usually, the slope of a line is calculated by dividing the difference in $Y (\Delta Y)$ by the difference in $X (\Delta X)$ between two points. To illustrate, consider the function $y = x^3$ at the point $(2.00, 8.00)$. The slope of the tangent line at the point could be approximated by calculating the slope of a line with points that are close to the point in question, $(2.00, 8.00)$. For instance, the slope of the line between points $(1.70, 4.91)$ and $(1.80, 5.83)$ is 9.2. Coming from the other end, the slope of the line between points $(2.30, 12.17)$ and $(2.40, 13.82)$ is 16.5. As the slope is calculated from points that are closer to the point in question, the slope approaches 12.0. Note that the slope cannot be calculated from a single point because the denominator in the slope equation equals zero.

Table 9. Slope of Lines Near the Point $(2.00, 8.00)$ *on* $y = x^3$

X	X^3	ΔX	ΔY	$\Delta Y / \Delta X$
1.50	3.38			
		0.10	0.72	7.2
1.60	4.10			
		0.10	0.82	8.2
1.70	4.91			
		0.10	0.92	9.2
1.80	5.83			
		0.10	1.03	10.3
1.90	6.86			
		0.10	1.14	11.4
2.00	8.00			
		0.10	1.26	12.6
2.10	9.26			
		0.10	1.39	13.9
2.20	10.65			
		0.10	1.52	15.2
2.30	12.17			
		0.10	1.65	16.5
2.40	13.82			
		0.10	1.80	18.01
2.50	15.63			

The slope of the tangent line at a point on the function can be determined using differential calculus by finding the derivative of the equation and evaluating it with x equaling the point in question. In this case, the original function is $y = x^3$, and its derivative is:

$$\frac{dy}{dx}(x^3) = 3x^2 + \text{constant}$$

Evaluating the derivative at $x = 2$ yields a value $(3)(2)^2 = 12$, which is the slope of the tangent at that point.

Example 4.

Thirty wells each generate $100,000 of profit, or $3,000,000 in total profit. We are considering adding wells to increase the total profit (TP). Because all wells draw from the same source, the profit of each well decreases by $1,000 for each additional well (AW). What number of wells maximizes total profit, and what is that profit? This scenario can be represented by the equation shown below.

$$TP = (30 + AW)(\$100,000 - \$1,000\,AW)$$

$$TP = \$3,000,000 - \$30,000\,AW + \$100,000\,AW - \$1,000\,AW^2$$

$$TP = -\$1,000\,AW^2 + \$70,000\,AW + \$3,000,000$$

This equation is shown in Figure 11. The maximum profit is at the peak of the curve, where the slope of the tangent line equals zero. It appears to be about $4,250,000.

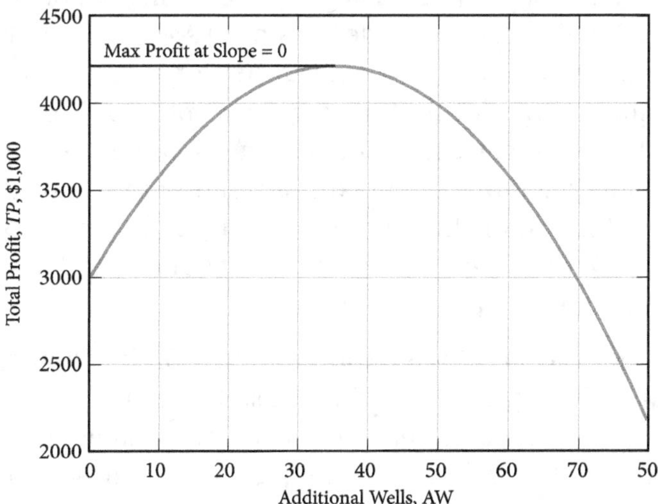

Figure 11. Maximize Well Profit

The derivative of the equation equals:

$$\frac{dTP}{dAW} = -2000\,AW + 70,000$$

The slope of a curve equals zero at a maximum or minimum. Setting the derivation to zero yields the maximum total profit.

$$-2,000\,AW + 70,000 = 0$$

$$AW = 35$$

With 35 additional wells, the total profit is calculated as follows:

$$TP = -\$1,000\,AW^2 + \$70,000\,AW + \$3,000,000$$

$$TP = -\$1,225,000 + \$2,450,000 + \$3,000,000 = \$4,225,000$$

1.4 Probability

Except in the most trivial of situations, engineering is probabilistic, meaning that the probability of an event occurring or not occurring is never 100%. Therefore, all designs have some probability, and it is essential to quantify that expectation of failure. It can then be determined if the level of failure is acceptable. Probability is calculated by analyzing a set of measured values. Usually, the first step is to calculate the maximum, minimum, range, mean, median, and mode of the data and create a histogram or other graphic to visualize the data. Then a probability model that best fits the data and situation is selected.

The most common and well-known model of probability is the normal or bell curve. It is widely used because much of the variation in nature and human characteristics and activity can be accurately modeled with it. An example of data whose probability of occurrence is usually modeled by a normal curve is intelligence quotient (IQ). A very large data set of scores have been measured over the years, and it is widely accepted that IQ measurements are normally distributed among the human population. Referring to Figure 12, the mean IQ of 100 is at the peak number of counts (occurrences); the curve is symmetric about the mean and is asymptotic (the curve never reaches zero at either tail) as you move away from the mean. The y-axis is either frequency of occurrence or count.

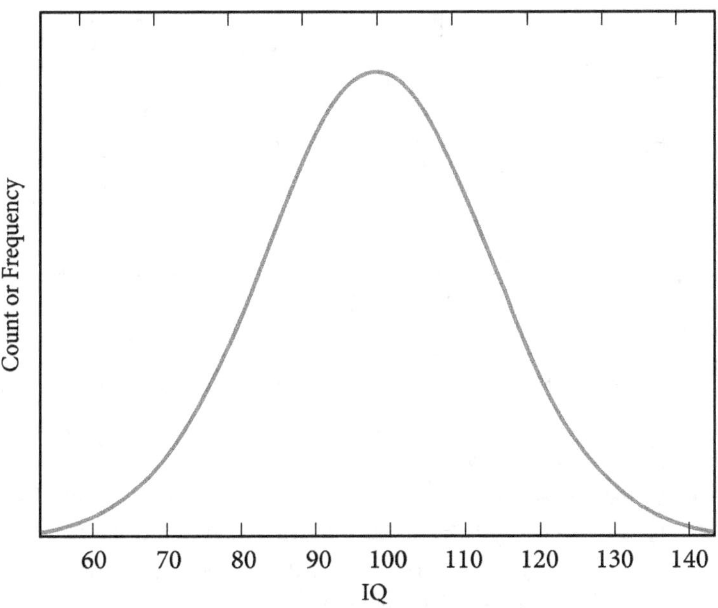

Figure 12. Normal Distribution of IQ

1.4.1 Histogram

As mentioned above, creating a histogram is a common early step in developing probabilities. The example shown here uses a data set of 100 randomly selected IQs to create a histogram, a series of vertical bars with a height equal to the number of measurements that fall within the bar's "bin" or width. In this case (see Figure 13), there are six bins each with a width of 15. Three measurements are between 55 and 70 in the first bin, 15 measurements are between 70 and 85, and so on. The sum of the counts in all bins equals the total number of measurements: 100. It is useful to create several histograms of the data with various bin

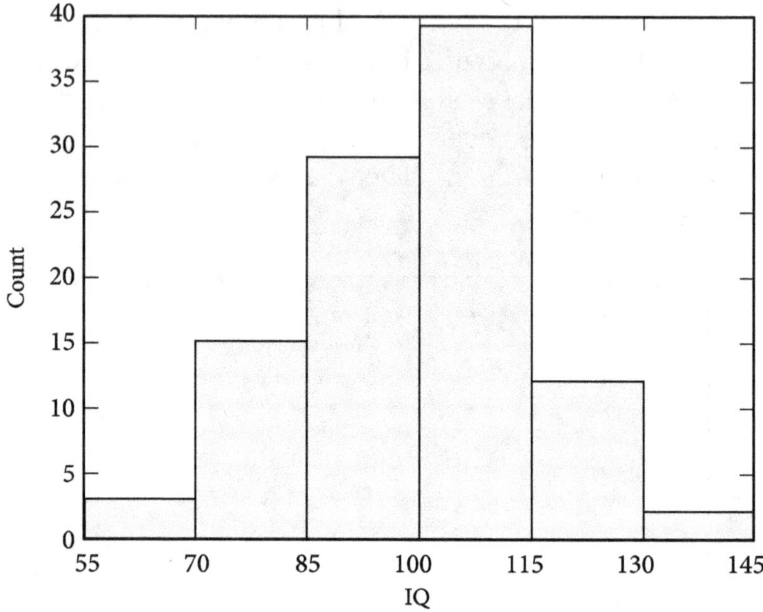

Figure 13. Histogram of 100 IQ Measurements

widths and observe the differences in shape. The general shape of this histogram is, as expected, similar to a normal curve where most IQ values are close to the mean and fewer IQ measurements occur at both the high and low ends.

1.4.2 Standard Deviation

We next "fit" the normal curve to the data. The number of a histogram's bins and the widths of the bins are finite. The normal curve has an infinite number of bins, and each bin width is infinitesimally small. To fit the normal curve, the mean and the standard deviation of the data are calculated. The standard deviation is a measure of the data's spread or central tendency.

Example 1.

To keep it simple, a small data set of five measurements will be used to demonstrate calculating standard deviation. Note that this is an unrealistically small sample set.

Small sample data set $= [4.0, 6.0, 7.0, 12.0, 15.0]$

Standard deviation is traditionally labeled as σ (sigma); however, this book also uses the term SD. Equation (1.2) is the equation for sample standard deviation, where a sample is a subset of the entire population of a full set of data. The equation for the standard deviation of the entire population differs only in that the denominator is simply N, not $N-1$. With large data sets, using N rather than $N-1$ makes little difference; however, with a small number of measurements, the difference is significant. Most data sets in engineering are a large sample of the entire population. Note that the units of the standard deviation and the measurements are the same.

$$\sigma = \sqrt{\frac{1}{N-1} \sum_{i=1}^{N} (x_i - \overline{x})^2} \qquad (1.2)$$

- N is the number of data points

- x_i is the value of a single data point

- Σ (uppercase sigma) indicates summation starting with the first value and ending with the Nth value

- $\overline{x}$ (x-bar) is the mean of the data set

In this case:

$$\overline{x} = 8.8$$

$$N = 5$$

$$\sum_{i=1}^{N} (x_i - \overline{x})^2 = (4.0 - 8.8)^2 + (6.0 - 8.8)^2$$

$$+ (7.0 - 8.8)^2 + (12.0 - 8.8)^2 + (15.0 - 8.8)^2 = 82.8.$$

$$\sigma = \sqrt{\frac{1}{4}(82.8)} = 4.55$$

1.4.3 Normal Curve

A normal curve is a distribution of values that takes the shape of what is often referred to as a bell curve, as mentioned in the previous section. The entire area under a normal curve is one, meaning the probability is 100%.

The equation of the normal curve is shown in equation (1.3).

$$f(x) = \frac{1}{\sqrt{2\pi\sigma^2}} e^{-\frac{(x-\overline{x})^2}{2\sigma^2}} \tag{1.3}$$

e is the value of the natural log(2.718)

$\overline{x}$ is the mean

σ is the standard deviation

> **Example 2.**
>
> To illustrate the creation of a normal curve, assume a scenario where a manufacturer produces parts that are designed to be 22 mm in length. To evaluate the precision of the fabrication of these parts, a large sample of produced parts is measured. The measurements result in a mean value of 22 mm and standard deviation of 2.0 mm.
>
> Figure 14 shows the distribution of measured part lengths created by the existing manufacturing process. Note that the y-axis is a count of the measurements. The upper x-axis shows the value of a measurement. As expected, the curve shows that the part lengths will tend to cluster near the mean, and as you move right or left from the mean, there are fewer parts with those measurements.
>
> The lower x-axis is the value of the standard deviation that corresponds to the measurement above. For instance, 18 mm is two standard deviations to the left (-2σ) of the mean,

and 24 mm is one standard deviation to the right $(+1\sigma)$ of the mean.

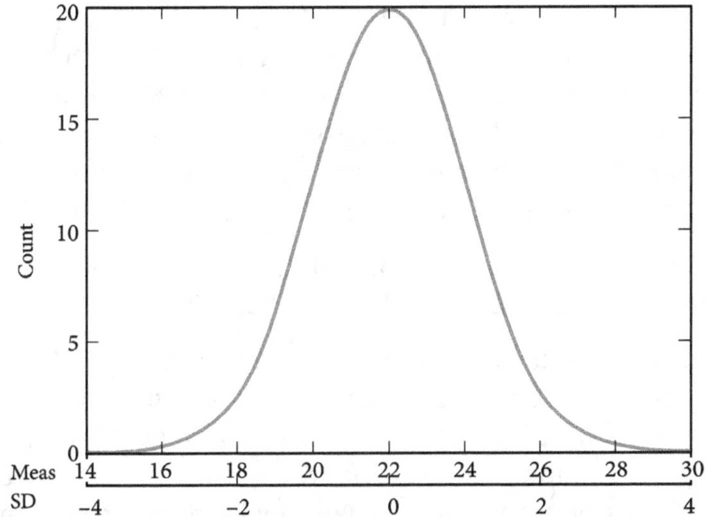

Figure 14. Example of Measurements and Standard Deviations

Probability is the area under the curve between any two measurements, including $\pm\infty$ (infinity). Reviewing the construction of a histogram may help to understand why.

The manufacturer can now quantify the precision of the manufacturing process. The goal is to create parts that are 22 mm in length, but it is impossible to create anything exactly any measurement. Every part will be less than or greater than 22 mm by some amount. Even if it were possible to produce a part exactly 22 mm long, it would be impossible to verify with a measurement. A measurement is also never exact, and it is essential that the engineer understand this. It logically follows, then, that an engineering specification cannot require an exact dimension; it must state an acceptable tolerance, or range, of the dimension. To express the desired lengths of this inexact process requires probability.

With a normal curve established, probabilities can be evaluated. The six curves in Figure 15 show the probabilities (area beneath the curve) of a measurement occurring between standard deviations, or from standard deviations to $\pm\infty$.

Figure 15(a) shows that the probability of a measurement occurring between the mean and -1σ is 34%. Because the curve is symmetric about the mean, the probability of a measurement occurring between the mean and $+1\sigma$ is also 34%. In other words, there is a 68% chance that the length of any single part is between 20 mm and 24 mm. When communicating this, it would typically be stated that the length of the part is 22 mm $\pm$2.0 mm (68%).

Figure 15(b) shows the probability of any single part length being between $-1SD$ and $-2SD$, which is about 14%.

Figure 15(c) illustrates the probability of a part length being less than 18 mm ($-2SD$) as 2%. This is equivalent to calculating the probability of it being greater than 18 mm as 98% using the following calculation, knowing that the probability of a measurement occurring between one standard deviation and two standard deviations is 14%.

14% ($-2SD$ to $-1SD$) plus 34% ($-1SD$ to mean) plus 50% (mean to + infinity) = 98%

Likewise, the probability between two and three standard deviations is 2%. Beyond three standard deviations, probabilities quickly become small.

Figure 15(d) figure shows that the probability of a part being less than 3 SDs from the mean (less than 16 mm) is 0.13%.

Figure 15(e) simply shows the area between plus and minus one standard deviation is 68% (34% plus 34%).

Figure 15(f) shows that the probability of a measurement occurring to be either greater or less than two standard deviations is 4.6% (2.3% plus 2.3%). The is similar to Figure 15(c) because one the limits is infinity rather than a standard deviation or fixed measurement.

It is worth memorizing the approximate probabilities between the first few standard deviations.

- Between 0σ and $1\sigma = 34\%$
- Between 1σ and $2\sigma = 14\%$
- Between 2σ and $3\sigma = \ \ 2\%$

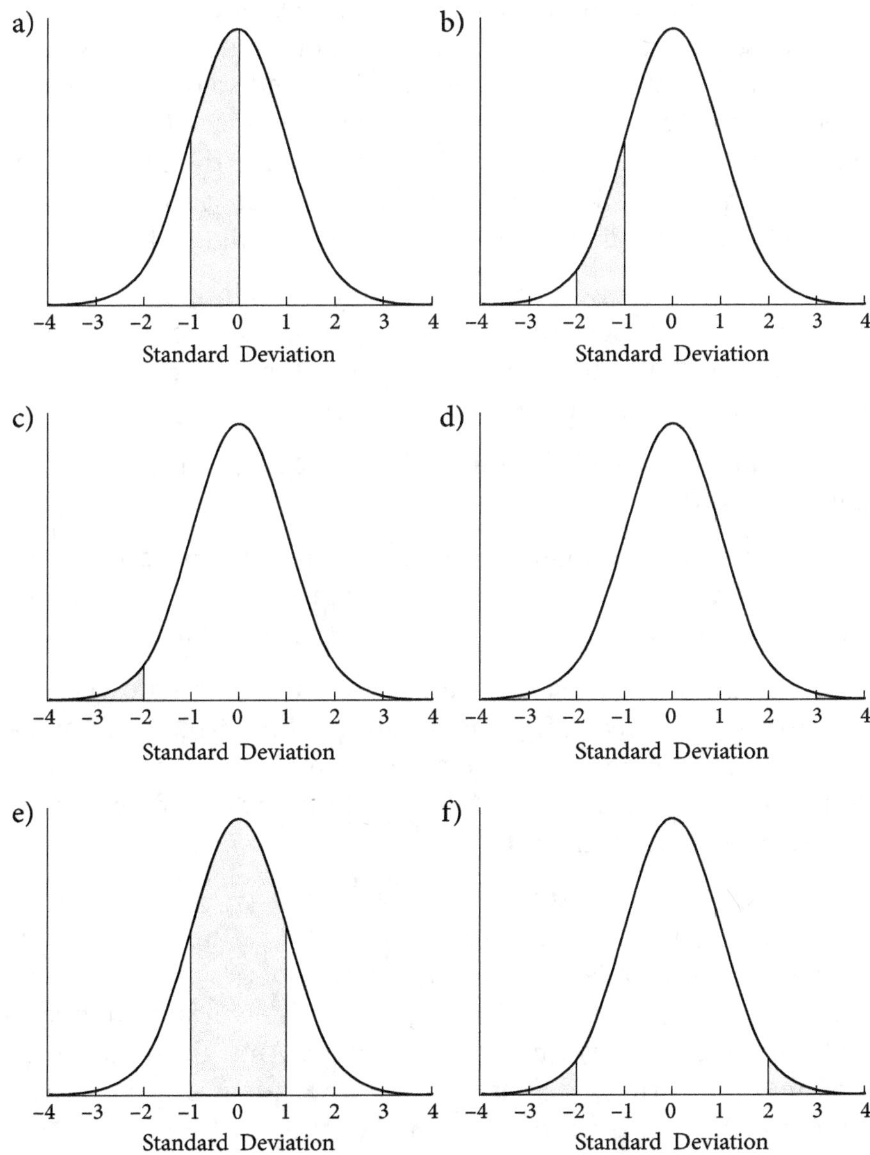

Figure 15. Probabilities between Standard Deviations

An explanation of why the probability of any single measurement is zero is that probabilities are the area beneath the curve. The area beneath a single measurement is a line, and the area of a line is zero; therefore, the probability is zero.

As noted above, measurements are finite in their precision where precision is typically indicated by the number of digits. Consider measuring the length of an object. It could be measured as 5 m. More precisely, at 5.3 m, 5.34 m, 5.342 m, and so on. Each measured length is correct—differing only in precision. The precision to which a measurement is taken is determined by the capability of the measuring instrument, skill of the technician, time and effort required, and most importantly, the purpose of the measurement.

Much of the art of engineering is in understanding the required precision for its purpose. If the measurement is not precise enough, the need is not met. If the measurement is too precise, it is likely that time, money, or expertise was wasted.

In summary, critical characteristics of probability and measurements are as follows:

- A measurement can never be exact. In the example above, the measurement can be taken to ever-increasing levels of precision, but no single level of precision is *the* measurement.

- The value of a measurement will always be unknown and unknowable. Measuring the length of the object to an ever-increasing precision eventually leads to measuring at the molecular and then atomic level. At some point, the act of measuring alters the measurement itself.

- In working with measurements, precision is typically indicated by the number of digits. It is a statement of the level of confidence the engineer has in the precision of the measurement, and therefore, in the solution. Again, we are typically confident of a number to only three or four digits. An eight-digit result of an engineering calculation would represent either incredible precision of the measurements or the inexperience of the engineer presenting the results.

With measurements as its foundation, engineering typically expresses solutions probabilistically. If asked for the length of an object, the technically correct answer is that it's unknowable, but that is not a useful answer. A correct and useful answer is to present the result within a range along with the associated probability. For instance, the length of an object may be stated as between 5.61 m and 5.65 m with 95% confidence, and it would typically be written as 5.63 m $\pm$ 0.02 m (95%). To calculate probability, repeated measurements are needed, and a greater number of measurements will result in a lower SD and higher confidence. It is important to note that, in practice, measurements and their precision are often explicitly known and accepted because of long experience and accepted practice.

In the example above, probabilities were found using the area under full standard deviations. To find the area beneath the curve between values that are at partial standard deviations, the integral of the equation of the normal curve must be determined. Working with the integral is difficult and typically left to a computer or calculator. Without those, a table of "Z-scores" can be used. The relationship of probability, Z-score, SD, and the value in question is shown in Equation (1.4). The relationship between the Z-score and probability is shown in the Z-table, Table 10.

$$Z = \frac{x - \overline{x}}{SD} \tag{1.4}$$

Table 10. Z-score Probabilities

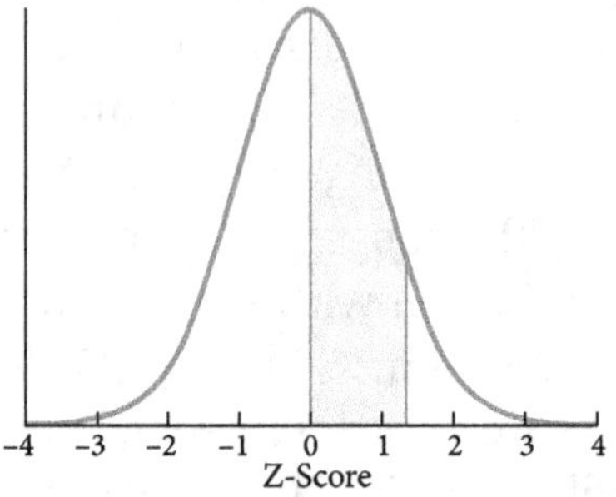

Z	0	0.01	0.02	0.03	0.04	0.05	0.06	0.07	0.08	0.09
0.0	0.0000	0.0040	0.0080	0.0120	0.0160	0.0199	0.0239	0.0279	0.0319	0.0359
0.1	0.0398	0.0438	0.0478	0.0517	0.0557	0.0596	0.0636	0.0675	0.0714	0.0753
0.2	0.0793	0.0832	0.0871	0.0910	0.0948	0.0987	0.1026	0.1064	0.1103	0.1141
0.3	0.1179	0.1217	0.1255	0.1293	0.1331	0.1368	0.1406	0.1443	0.1480	0.1517
0.4	0.1554	0.1591	0.1628	0.1664	0.1700	0.1736	0.1772	0.1808	0.1844	0.1879
0.5	0.1915	0.1950	0.1985	0.2019	0.2054	0.2088	0.2123	0.2157	0.2190	0.2224
0.6	0.2257	0.2291	0.2324	0.2357	0.2389	0.2422	0.2454	0.2486	0.2517	0.2549
0.7	0.2580	0.2611	0.2642	0.2673	0.2704	0.2734	0.2764	0.2794	0.2823	0.2852
0.8	0.2881	0.2910	0.2939	0.2967	0.2995	0.3023	0.3051	0.3078	0.3106	0.3133
0.9	0.3159	0.3186	0.3212	0.3238	0.3264	0.3289	0.3315	0.3340	0.3365	0.3389
1.0	0.3413	0.3438	0.3461	0.3485	0.3508	0.3531	0.3554	0.3577	0.3599	0.3621
1.1	0.3643	0.3665	0.3686	0.3708	0.3729	0.3749	0.3770	0.3790	0.3810	0.3830
1.2	0.3849	0.3869	0.3888	0.3907	0.3925	0.3944	0.3962	0.3980	0.3997	0.4015
1.3	0.4032	0.4049	0.4066	0.4082	0.4099	0.4115	0.4131	0.4147	0.4162	0.4177
1.4	0.4192	0.4207	0.4222	0.4236	0.4251	0.4265	0.4279	0.4292	0.4306	0.4319
1.5	0.4332	0.4345	0.4357	0.4370	0.4382	0.4394	0.4406	0.4418	0.4429	0.4441
1.6	0.4452	0.4463	0.4474	0.4484	0.4495	0.4505	0.4515	0.4525	0.4535	0.4545
1.7	0.4554	0.4564	0.4573	0.4582	0.4591	0.4599	0.4608	0.4616	0.4625	0.4633
1.8	0.4641	0.4649	0.4656	0.4664	0.4671	0.4678	0.4686	0.4693	0.4699	0.4706
1.9	0.4713	0.4719	0.4726	0.4732	0.4738	0.4744	0.4750	0.4756	0.4761	0.4767
2.0	0.4772	0.4778	0.4783	0.4788	0.4793	0.4798	0.4803	0.4808	0.4812	0.4817
2.1	0.4821	0.4826	0.4830	0.4834	0.4838	0.4842	0.4846	0.4850	0.4854	0.4857
2.2	0.4861	0.4864	0.4868	0.4871	0.4875	0.4878	0.4881	0.4884	0.4887	0.4890
2.3	0.4893	0.4896	0.4898	0.4901	0.4904	0.4906	0.4909	0.4911	0.4913	0.4916
2.4	0.4918	0.4920	0.4922	0.4925	0.4927	0.4929	0.4931	0.4932	0.4934	0.4936
2.5	0.4938	0.4940	0.4941	0.4943	0.4945	0.4946	0.4948	0.4949	0.4951	0.4952
2.6	0.4953	0.4955	0.4956	0.4957	0.4959	0.4960	0.4961	0.4962	0.4963	0.4964
2.7	0.4965	0.4966	0.4967	0.4968	0.4969	0.4970	0.4971	0.4972	0.4973	0.4974
2.8	0.4974	0.4975	0.4976	0.4977	0.4977	0.4978	0.4979	0.4979	0.4980	0.4981
2.9	0.4981	0.4982	0.4982	0.4983	0.4984	0.4984	0.4985	0.4985	0.4986	0.4986
3.0	0.4987	0.4987	0.4987	0.4988	0.4988	0.4989	0.4989	0.4989	0.4990	0.4990

Example 3.

Returning to IQ and its normal distribution as an example, the mean is 100, and the standard deviation is 15. Use the Z-table to find the probability that a person's IQ is greater than 120. First, calculate the Z-score for 120. Use Equation (1.4) to determine the appropriate Z-score.

$$Z = \frac{120 - 100}{15} = 1.33$$

A Z-score of 1.33 corresponds to a probability of 40.8% as shown Table 10. This is found by locating 1.3 on the leftmost column and using that row to find the value under 0.03 ($1.3 + 0.03 = 1.33$). 40.8% makes sense because the probability between the mean and $+1SD$ is 34%, and the probability between the mean and $+2SD$ is about 48%, so a Z-score between 1 and 2 would have a probability between 34% and 48%. When using the Z-table, note that the graphic indicates that the probabilities in the table are from $Z = 0$ to a positive Z. Therefore the maximum probability shown is nearly 50%.

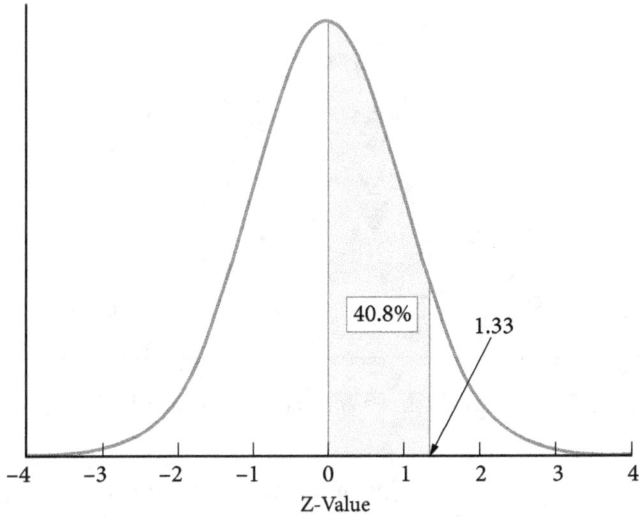

Figure 16. Probability IQ Greater Than 120

Using the *Z*-table value of 40.8%, the probability of a person having an IQ greater than 120 (Figure 16) is 9.2%. This is because the area (probability) that you are looking for is that to the right of $Z = 1.33$.

Area under entire curve = 100%. Area left of the mean = 50%. Shaded area = 40.8%.

$$\text{Solution} = 100\% - 50\% - 40.8\% = 9.2\%$$

Because the curve is symmetric, although the *Z*-score of a measurement less than the mean is negative, the same *Z*-table can be used. For instance, what is the probability that a person's IQ is less than 95?

An IQ of 95 results in $Z = -0.333$, and the table shows a probability of about 13.0%. Looking at the graphic, 13.0% is the probability between the mean and 95. Therefore, the probability of an IQ less than 95 is: $50\% - 13\%$, which equals 37%.

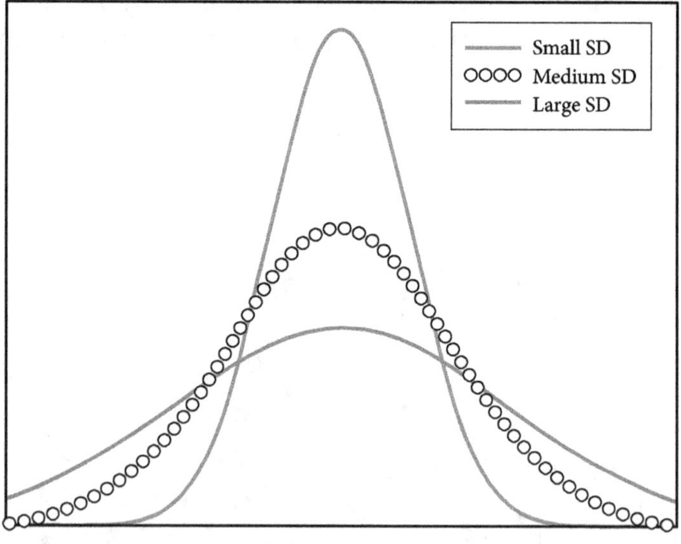

Figure 17. Normal Curve Shape and Standard Deviation

Figure 17 illustrates the effect of standard deviation on the spread of the curve. The values on the *x*-axis remain the same. A large standard deviation is flattened, spreading more area (probability) over a given range of measurements. In comparison, a small standard deviation places a large area over a lessor measurement range. A smaller deviation will result in less area at the tails and more toward the mean.

Example 4.

A manufacturer is machining metal cylinders with a design diameter of 0.50 in and an acceptable tolerance of ±0.03 in. A large number of test cylinders were produced to measure their diameters when created with existing machines and techniques. It was found that the mean diameter was 0.50 in and standard deviation 0.02 in. Without changes to machinery or production technique, 6.7% of the parts would be too small. This is because at $x = 0.47$ in, $Z = -1.5$, giving a probability of 43.3% left of the mean, leaving 6.7% to the left of $Z = 1.5$. Symmetry says 6.7% would be too large, so a total of 13.4% would fail. See Figure 18.

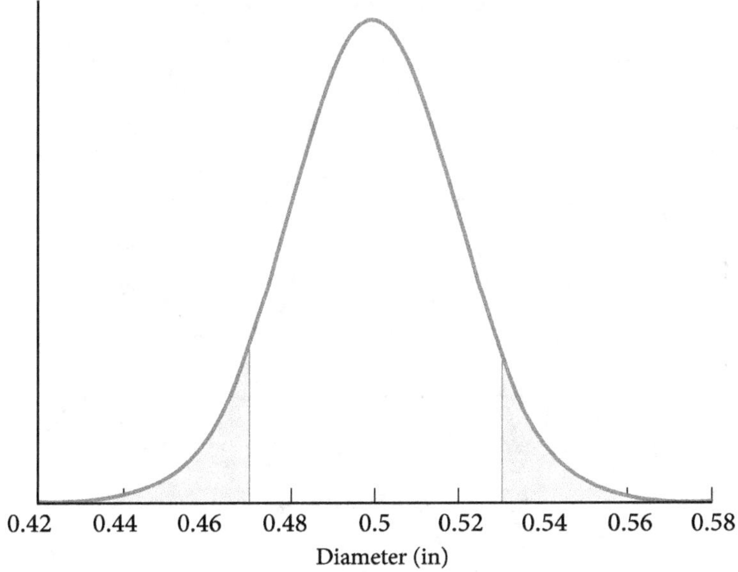

Figure 18. SD = 0.20 in

The manufacturer determines that a 97% acceptance rate is necessary. To determine the required SD, use the Z-table to find the *Z*-score for 48.5%. The expectation is that 1.5% of parts would be too small and 1.5% of parts would be too large. The mean remains 0.50 in; the maximum length = 0.53 in, and the minimum length equals 0.47 in. The *Z*-table shows a *Z*-score of 2.17, for 48.5%.

Rearrange Equation (1.4) and consider only the right tail of 1.5% where the diameters are greater than 0.53 in (lengths between 0.50 and 0.53) and the required $SD = 0.014$ in.

$$S = \frac{x - \overline{x}}{Z} = \frac{0.53 - 0.50}{2.17} = 0.014 \text{ in}$$

Note that Figure 18 has a larger SD: therefore, a broader spread and lower peak than Figure 19.

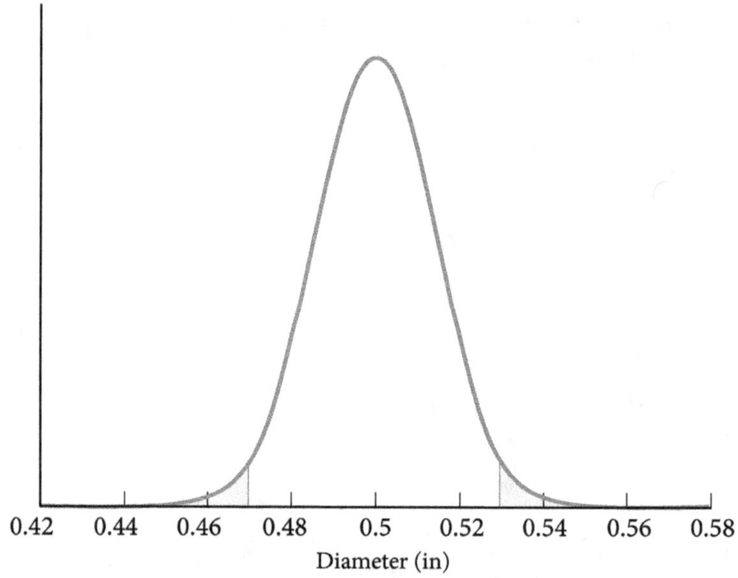

Figure 19. SD = 0.14 in

2

Relationships

Lord Kelvin

2.1 Cause and Effect

Essentially, prediction is the purpose of engineering. A typical analysis measures an initial action and then measures the effect. That reaction provides the engineer with insight into cause and effect. For instance, a structural beam is designed to support a certain weight. When that weight is placed on the beam, it should then deflect to the calculated value. When predicting cause and effect (relationships), it is important to clearly define the cause and its resulting effect; it is not always obvious. Cause is the independent variable and plotted on the x-axis, and effect is the dependent variable, plotted on the y-axis.

Before looking at the mathematics of relationships, we must first be sure to understand the difference between correlation and causation. As a simple example, when you note both the position of the sun in the sky and the time of day many times, you'll find that it correlates very well. The sun moves a certain amount during the first hour of a day and continues to move the same amount each hour thereafter. The movement of your watch's hour hand correlates nicely with the movement of the sun. After a number of measurements, you could predict the position of the sun by reading your watch. With correlation established, the next step is to look at possible causation. Is it the movement of the sun that advances the hands on your watch? Or is it the advancement of time that results in the different position of the sun? Obviously, the latter is the case. So, the position of the sun is correlated to the reading of your watch, but it is not caused by the position of the watch hand. It is quite often useful to establish correlation while aware that it is not necessarily causal. Causality is often difficult to establish, and when it's found to exist, it is most often only partially causal with other factors affecting the relationship.

2.2 Three Common Relationships

Finding relationships between phenomena leads to an understanding of apparent cause and effect used in prediction. We will look at three common types of relationships: linear, power, and exponential.

Linear:

$$y = mx + b \tag{2.1}$$

Power:

$$y = kx^m \tag{2.2}$$

Exponential:

$$y = ke^{mx} \tag{2.3}$$

Table 11 summarizes the equations of these three functions in both their common and linear form.

Table 11. Common Relationships

Type	Common	Linear	Constants	Notes
Linear	$y = mx + b$	$y = mx + b$	$m = \dfrac{(y_2 - y_1)}{(x_2 - x_1)}$ $b = y_2 - mx_2$	Plots straight on rectilinear paper.
Power	$y = kx^m$	$\log(y) = m\log(x) + \log(k)$	$m = \dfrac{\log(y_2) - \log(y_1)}{\log(x_2) - \log(x_1)}$ $k = \dfrac{y_2}{x_2^m}$	Plots straight on log-log paper.
Exponential	$y = ke^{mx}$	$\ln(y) = mx + \ln(k)$	$m = \dfrac{\ln(y_2) - \ln(y_1)}{x_2 - x_1}$ $k = \dfrac{y_2}{e^{mx_2}}$	Plots straight on semi-log y axis.

Again, it is not always obvious—but it is extremely important—to be clear what drives the relationship (independent variable) and its effect (dependent variable). When time is one of the variables, it is usually the independent variable because the passage of time is constant and does not depend on anything else.

2.2.1 Linear Relationships

As a simple example of determining a relationship, you can measure distance traveled over a period of time and plot the results on a rectilinear grid. The data is in Table 12 and Figure 20.

Table 12. Linear Data

Time (s)	Distance (m)
2	5.1
4	12.1
6	17.5
8	24.2

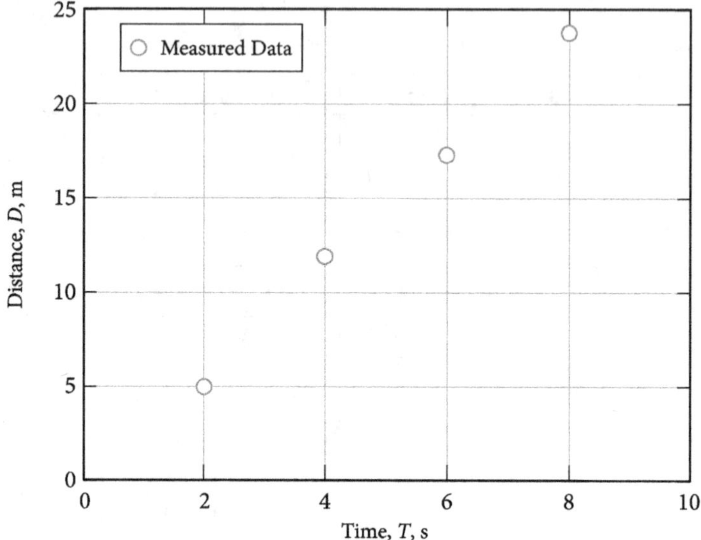

Figure 20. Plot of Linear Data

The data plotted in Figure 20 appears to follow a straight line on a rectilinear graph, meaning it is most likely a linear relationship with the general form $y = mx + b$. Using the variables of this specific case, its form is $D = mT + b$, where distance (D) is the dependent variable and time (T) is the independent variable. In other words, time is the independent variable because it proceeds at a constant rate and is the value from which you measure the dependent variable of distance.

A straight edge would show that while the points tend to follow a straight line, they do not form a perfectly straight line. Using the data, a line of best fit (LBF) can be calculated. One way to find the equation of a LBF is by the method of selected points. First, draw, by eye, what appears to be the line of best fit. Next, select two points on the line that are not original data points and that are within the extremes of the data. Then calculate the coefficients using Equation (2.1).

Referring to Figure 21, the two points selected are $(6.7, 20)$ and $(3.5, 10)$. Using Equation (2.1), $b = -0.94$ and $m = 3.12$. The equation of the LBF is $D = 3.12T - 0.94$.

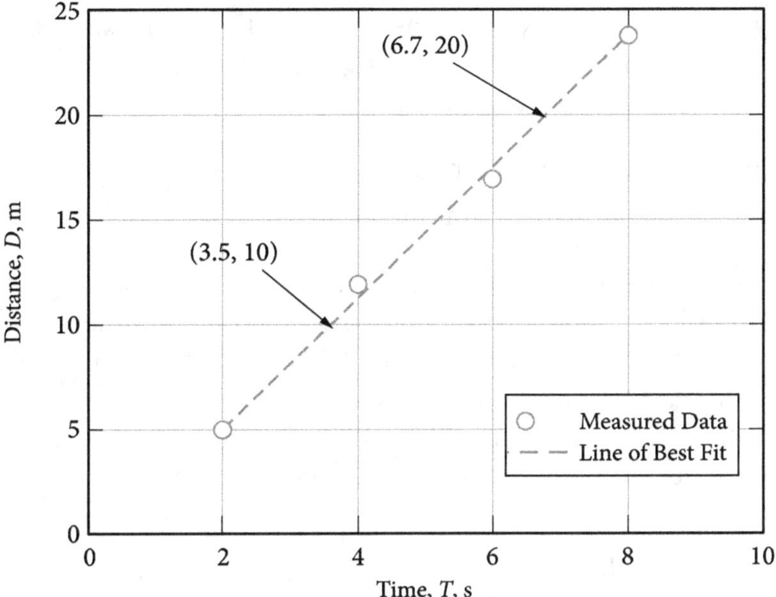

Figure 21. Selected Points on Linear Line of Best Fit

A more common way of calculating the LBF is the method of least squares. This mathematical procedure minimizes the sum of the squared vertical distances between each point and the LBF. This is a cumbersome calculation, best solved with a calculator or computer. Using the method of least squares in a computer program, the slope and intercept of the LBF are: $m = 3.14$ and $b = -0.94$, or $D = 3.14T - 0.94$.

In this case, it could be argued that there is a fifth point at $(0, 0)$ because of the nature of the experiment, but we will continue without.

2.2.2 Logarithmic Graphing Background

One purpose logarithms serve is to more easily work with large numbers for both calculating and graphing. Essentially, logarithms express numbers with inverse exponents. For example, $4^3 = 64$ because $(4)(4)(4) = 64$. So, the log of 64 to the base of 4 equals 3. It would be written $\log_4(64) = 3$. The two most common bases of logs are 10 and e (2.71). When you see the expression $\log(x)$, it is assumed the base is 10, unless specified otherwise. Examples are:

$$\log_{10}(1000) = 3, \quad \text{commonly written} \quad \log(1000) = 3$$
$$\log_e(1500) = 7.3, \quad \text{commonly written} \quad \ln(1500) = 7.3$$

As an example of plotting numbers as logs, consider the growth of money in a bank account as shown in the example in Table 13. The scenario is that you deposit $100.00 in an account and then observe the balance of money in the account every two years. Using this data, you want to determine the equation that predicts the amount of money in your account at any time.

Table 13. Growth of Money over Time

Year	Balance	Natural Log of Balance
0	$ 100.00	4.605
2	$ 134.99	4.905
4	$ 182.21	5.205
6	$ 245.96	5.505
8	$ 332.01	5.805
10	$ 448.17	6.105
12	$ 604.96	6.405
14	$ 816.62	6.705
16	$1,102.32	7.005
18	$1,487.97	7.305
20	$2,008.55	7.605

The data in Table 13 is plotted in Figure 22. When plotted on rectilinear paper, the balance-over-time curve is not straight. However, plotting the log of the balance on a rectilinear graph is a straight line. The data was linearized by taking the natural log of the balance. Because the data is linearized, it will plot straight on a rectilinear scale.

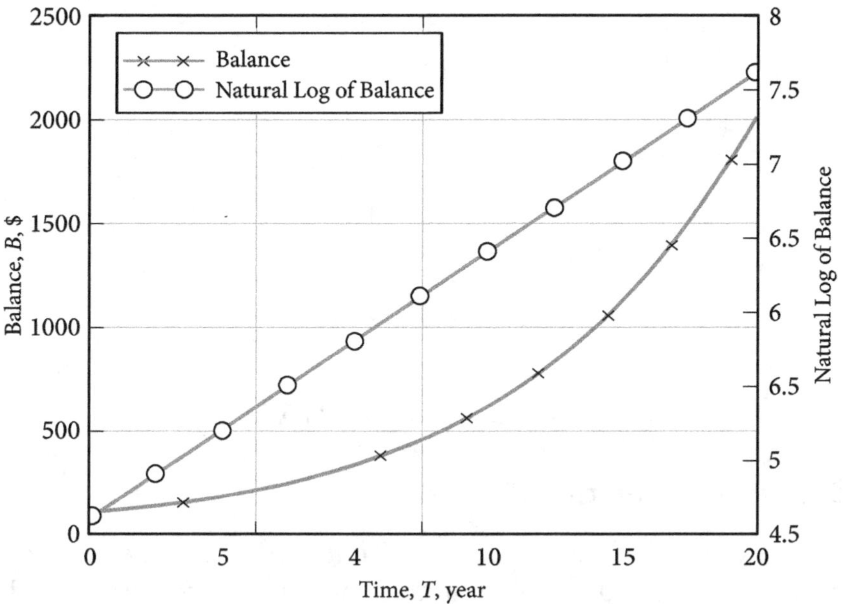

Figure 22. Plot of Balances and Their Logs

Another way to represent non-linear data as linear is to plot it using a log or semi-log scale. The general equation for the growth of money shown in Table 13 is an exponential function with the general form of $y = ke^{mx}$, and in this case, it is $B = Pe^{rT}$, where B is the amount in the account at any given time, P is the principal or beginning balance ($100.00), r is the interest rate, and T is the time since the account was opened in years. Because the relationship is exponential, we will plot the balances on a semi-log scale where the data appears straight, confirming that it is an exponential relationship.

In this instance, the method of least squares was used to calculate the function as $B = 100e^{0.15T}$. This means that the annual interest rate is 15%, compounded continuously.

To ensure that you can read a logarithmic scale, verify the plotting of each point in Figure 23.

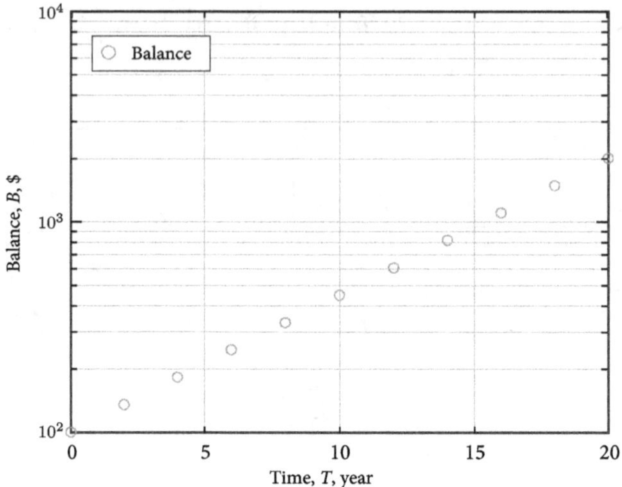

Figure 23. Semi-log Function Plot of Balances

2.2.3 Power Relationships

As an example of using measured data to determine a power function, imagine drawing a number of circles with varying radii on grid paper and then measuring the area of each circle. The unit of radius is the length of a side of a grid's square, and the unit of area are the number of squares within the circle. The results are as follows:

Table 14. Area of Circles with Varying Radii

Radius, R, side length	Measured Area, A, squares
1.0	3
3.0	26
5.0	76
7.0	157
9.0	254
11.0	390
13.0	550

The data is first plotted on rectilinear paper as shown in Figure 24. The data points do not form a straight line, indicating a non-linear function.

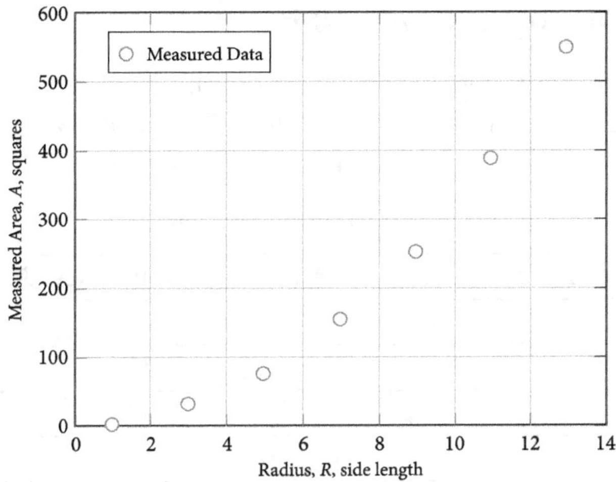

Figure 24. Power Function on a Rectilinear Grid

Next, the data is plotted on log-log paper (see Figure 25), where it appears to be a straight line, indicating that the relationship between radius and area is a power function in the form of $y = kx^m$. In this instance, the method of least squares was used to calculate the coefficients of k and m, resulting in the function $A = 3.241R^{1.989}$, which is very close to the known relationship used to calculate the area of a circle.

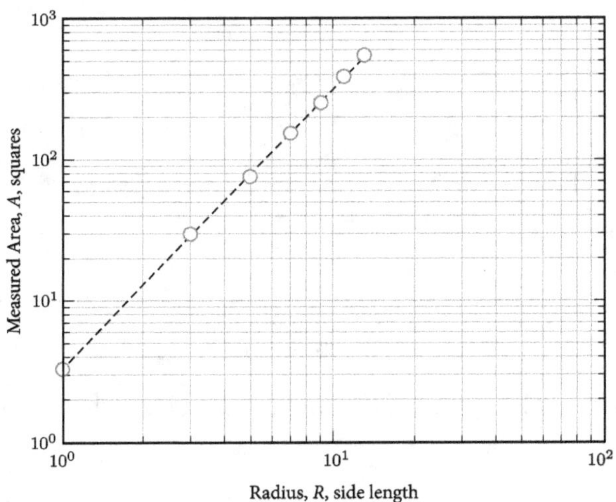

Figure 25. Power Function on a log-log Plot

2.2.4 Exponential Relationships

To experimentally determine an exponential function, we'll measure the decay of a substance over time. The results are as follows.

Table 15. Decay over Time

Time, T, day	Amount of substance, A, mg
0	100
1	48
2	27
3	13
4	7.0
5	2.8

Plotting the data on rectilinear paper as shown in Figure 26 does not produce a straight line, so the relationship is not linear.

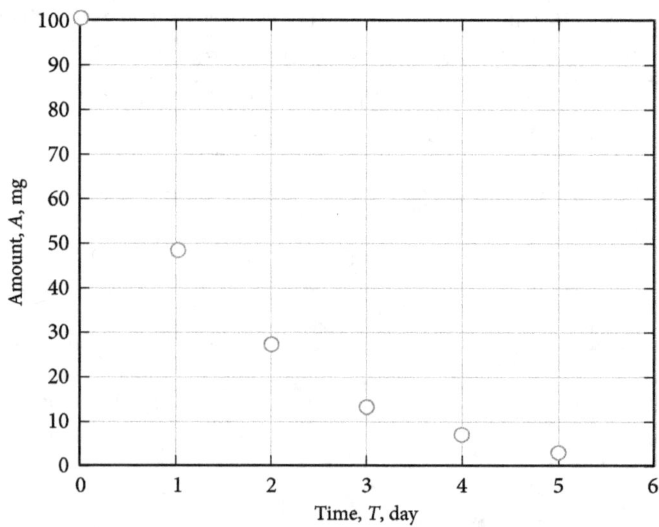

Figure 26. Exponential Function on a Rectilinear Grid

However, when the data is plotted on semi-log paper, it appears as a straight line (see Figure 27). The straight line suggests that the data fits an exponential function. Then, using the method of least squares, the constants are calculated as $k = 102$ and $m = 0.697$, which allows the relationship $A = 102e^{(-0.70T)}$ to be used to calculate the amount of the substance remaining at any given time.

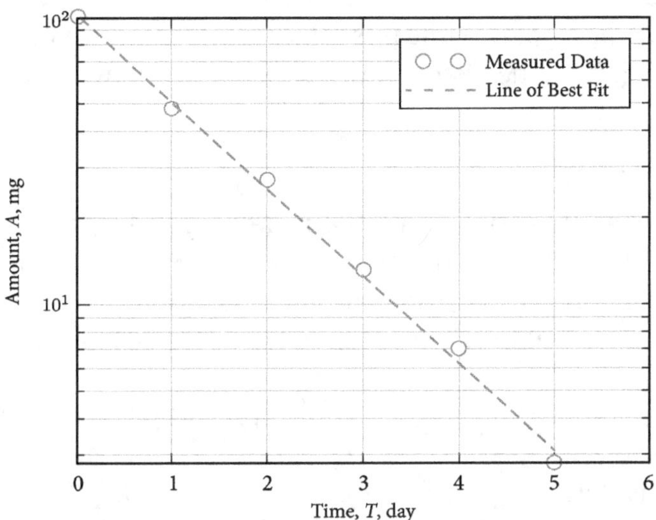

Figure 27. Exponential Function on a semi-log Plot

2.3 Theoretical and Empirical Equations

2.3.1 Theoretical

Design uses relationships to develop predictive models. As discussed below, we have fundamental principles that are the bedrock upon which our understanding of the physical world is based. Energy transfer, mechanics of materials, Ohm's law, and gravity are a few examples. Humans have always and are continuing to develop, improve, and use these relationships to solve problems. A generalization is that scientists develop these concepts, while engineers use them to create solutions to problems. The goal of the scientist is to advance our understanding of natural phenomena, and the goal of the engineer is to use this knowledge to create a useful design. If a design is not useful, it is not engineering.

A characteristic of a theoretical equation is that the units work. Perhaps the most famous theoretical equation is from Einstein's theory of special relativity that relates energy and mass: $e = mc^2$, where e is energy, m is mass, and c is the speed of light. The units work: mass times velocity squared equals energy. This is a fundamental concept that just is; it does not require any underlying principle. While this relationship was developed purely as theory, it has since been verified experimentally.

2.3.2 Empirical

An empirical equation is one that is developed by gathering data and, as shown above, developing a relationship by finding an equation that best fits the data. An example of an empirical relationship is Manning's equation which predicts flow in a natural channel

$$Q = (V)(A) = \left(\frac{1.49}{n} \right) AR^{0.67} S^{0.5}$$

where Q is flowrate ($[L]^3[T^{-1}]$), V is velocity ($[L][T]^{-1}$), A is the flow area ($[L]^2$), and S is slope ($[L][L]^{-1}$). The units make no sense. The units of the coefficient n are also senseless and used only to make the equation work. Units that don't work and a coefficient with the units needed to make it work is characteristic of an empirical equation. These equations are used when the physics are not understood. In this case, Manning's equation is used to predict the volumetric flowrate of water in a natural channel such as a river. Although flow in a river is commonplace, the physics of it, especially in the presence of turbulent flow, are not known well enough to develop a theoretic relationship. So, engineering can only measure such characteristics as slope, bed irregularities, and flow of many rivers and create an empirical equation with line fitting.

2.3.3 Mixed

For an airplane to fly, it must create an upward force called lift to counteract the downward force of its weight. Calculating the lift can be viewed as an application of Bernoulli's equation (Equation

(3.1); see also section 3.3.4) because as the wing moves through the air, the velocity of the air over the wing is greater than the velocity of the air beneath the wing. The result is that the pressure at the top of the wing is less than the pressure at the bottom of the wing. The net negative pressure at the top of the wing, multiplied by the wing area, results in a net force upward (lift). Assuming that the plane flies level, the upward force is equal to the weight of the plane. Bernoulli's equation, explained to a greater degree in the First Principles section, describes a flowing fluid and states that the sum of the velocity head, pressure head, and elevation head at one point is equal to the velocity head, pressure head, and elevation head at a second point along a streamline. Head is a unit common to velocity, pressure, and loss as length.

V is velocity, g is the acceleration due to gravity, P is pressure, γ is specific weight, and Z is elevation.

$$\frac{v_1^2}{2g} + \frac{P_1}{\gamma} + Z_1 - \text{Loss} = \frac{v_2^2}{2g} + \frac{P_2}{\gamma} + Z_2 \qquad (2.4)$$

In applying Bernoulli's equation, assume and deduce:

- Point 1 is at the bottom of the wing and point 2 at the top.

- The plane is flying level.

- No losses.

- $Z_1 = Z_2$. Thickness of the wing is negligible.

- P_1 is zero, therefore P_2 is negative.

- V_1 is zero, therefore V_2 is positive.

The equation reduces to:

$$0 = \frac{v_2^2}{2g} - \frac{P_2}{\gamma}$$

$$\frac{P}{\gamma} = \frac{v^2}{2g}$$

Recall that $\gamma = g\rho$

$$\frac{P}{g\rho} = \frac{v^2}{2g}$$

Multiply both sides by both g and ρ.

$$P = \rho\,\frac{v^2}{2}$$

Multiply both sides by the area of the top of the wing area (A), recalling that pressure multiplied by area equals force. In this case, the force is called lift. This is the theoretical equation used to calculate lift.

$$\text{Lift} = A\rho\,\frac{v^2}{2}$$

The textbook equation for lift is below, where the coefficient of lift (C_l) is added.

$$\text{Lift} = C_l A\rho\,\frac{v^2}{2}$$

Predicting lift is complicated. The theoretical Bernoulli's equation is useful to a degree, but not close enough. Experimental data fills the gap and is represented as the coefficient. In the case of aircraft, a wind tunnel could be used to measure the difference between the theoretical and actual lift. Complexities such as the air's viscosity, compressibility, and turbulence are not understood well enough to mathematically model, and an empirically derived coefficient is therefore needed to predict to the required accuracy.

3

Design

"Perfect is the Enemy of Good."

Voltaire

Engineering design is always a compromise, and the number of possible designs to solve a problem are infinite; therefore, no design is perfect. There are always trade-offs.

Not being able to have it all is often characterized as a choice of two out of three possibilities. For example, when designing batteries, you want them to be inexpensive, small, and have high energy storage. You can typically meet only two of the three criteria.

- Small and inexpensive batteries will have little energy storage.

- Small and high-storage batteries will be expensive.

- High-storage and inexpensive batteries will be large.

Another pick-two scenario might involve parts that are provided quickly, are inexpensive, and durable. Or software design in terms of being extensively tested, quickly developed, and robust.

An essential aspect of design is that cost is always a constraint to be minimized. An illustration of that is the joke that anybody can design a bridge that supports a load, but it takes an engineer to design a bridge that can *just barely* support a given load. Behind this joke is the concept that engineering design is constrained to perform to a certain level and no more. Doing more sounds "good," but it most often is not because overdesigning costs more in time, effort, money, and materials—all of which are scarce resources. If you'd like to know more, see the comment at the end of this section.

For instance, Blacksburg, Virginia receives about two feet of snow a year from about a dozen events. When designing a roof in Blacksburg, it would be ludicrous to design it with the ability to support the weight of 20 feet of snow. Designing the roof to support 20 feet of snow is good in the sense that it is possible that Blacksburg could receive a 20-foot snow event, but that is so improbable that the extra cost and resources to build it would not be justified. Further, if Blacksburg did happen to receive 20 feet of snow and the roof collapsed, that would be acceptable because the roof was not designed to support that weight, and the public implicitly understands the fact that any design is liable to fail under extreme circumstances.

The goal of engineering is that a design fails at an acceptable point. That acceptable point is determined through an often convoluted and inefficient process where politics, science, and engineering come together. Ultimately, society determines the acceptable level of failure. Standards of design are then developed by expert engineers, and it is those standards that guide the design.

If a design fails and the engineer is sued, the issue is not whether the engineer should have created a more robust design. The issue is whether the engineer's design was in keeping with the standards.

The joke mentioned in the discussion here is true in the sense that design always seeks efficiency in cost, materials, and time. What the drive for efficiency does not address is uncertainty.

As discussed, uncertainty is always present. Engineering design commonly accounts for this by applying factors of safety (FOS). Using a building as an example, design is a function of the loads to be supported and the method of support. Loads are typically designated as dead loads and live loads. Dead loads are those that are relatively constant, such as the weight of the structure itself, permanently installed equipment, and walls. Live loads are more variable weights to be borne by the building. Examples include people, movable equipment such as copiers, and furniture.

When designing a building, the engineer will follow standards published by authorities such as the European Union's Eurocode or the American Society of Civil Engineers. Calculated dead loads are multiplied by a factor of safety that is typically about 1.3, and live loads are multiplied by about 1.7. These factors of safety account for uncertainty in the actual capacity of structural support and anticipated use of the building. The FOS of dead loads are lower than the FOS of live loads because there is less uncertainty in dead load calculations. For dead loads, possible changes in the building's purpose over its design life are usually the largest uncertainty. Live load uncertainty is obviously greater because it's more likely to change.

Uncertainty in the support of the building is largely a function of materials. The carrying capacity of steel is relatively certain because of modern production methods and quality control, and it has a relatively low FOS, perhaps less than 1.1. Conversely, the FOS of wood structural members and ground support have greater uncertainty and correspondingly larger factors of safety.

Factors of safety are also a function of the purpose of structure. For instance, the failure of a highway bridge could be catastrophic in terms of lives lost and the cost of alternative transportation. It warrants a large factor of safety. On the other hand, advances in the methods and materials used in the production of structural steel, for example, could lower the uncertainty of its carrying capacity, which would result in a lower factor of safety and lower the cost of the structure.

3.1 Opportunity Cost

The duty of the engineer is to serve society, and society has more problems than resources to solve them. As discussed above, every dollar spent, hour worked, and bit of material consumed could be used elsewhere. Opportunity cost is the idea of evaluating the *best* use of scarce resources. For example, in each person's private life, opportunity cost is evaluated, very often implicitly, as each dollar, which is a scarce resource, is spent. In deciding to eat lunch at a restaurant with other office staff and spend $15.00 extra dollars above the cost of a homemade meal, the spender is saying that, at that moment, the best use of the $15.00 is the convenience and pleasure of eating with colleagues. The decision implies this is better use of the money than putting it toward retirement, giving to charity, saving for a new car, or any number of other possible uses. Likewise, when a government builds a $10,000,000 water treatment plant, it is forgoing $10,000,000 of potential transportation improvements, health-care research, creation of a reserve fund, lower taxes, or any number of other uses that would benefit society. Making the decision to build that water treatment plant should come with the explicit agreement that this is the *best* use of the money. The potential *good* uses of scarce resources are infinite, meaning that it is impossible to evaluate all alternatives. However, there should still be an attempt to find the *best* design. The concept of opportunity cost is directly related to the concept of designing to a standard of good enough discussed above, and it also supports solving problems to a specified level of function and no more.

While it is good that a roof can withstand an extremely large and improbable weather event, it is not good that excessive scarce resources were used in its construction. It is usually easy to find a good solution to a problem. However, engineering requires an attempt to find the best solution. There is a problem, however, because essentially innumerable solutions are possible, and finding the best is difficult, perhaps even impossible.

3.2 Marginal Design

The knowledge and skills required of engineering design are taken from engineers before us. Previous generations of practitioners have developed relationships, materials, methods of analyses, processes, and procedures that current engineers expand, improve, and use in new ways to better solve problems. It is essential that engineers are first able to understand and apply this knowledge in its current setting before they can then take this knowledge and apply it in new ways to solve new problems, or old problems in new ways. A solid grounding in these first principles and their conventual applications is needed to improve current designs and develop new engineering practices. For example, thermodynamics and its traditional applications must be well understood before they can be applied to new problems of heat transfer.

Figure 28 represents a hypothetical situation of the time an engineer uses to develop a new design or process to maximize a client's profit. This is a simplified scenario used only to demonstrate designing on the margin. The example has three basic phases. The first involves understanding the problem and considering the fundamental principles that may be useful in creating a solution. The second phase is where the engineer's time and resources rapidly increase the profit. This phase could be viewed as typical production of a competent engineer. The third phase of the design is where it is increasingly difficult to improve the design.

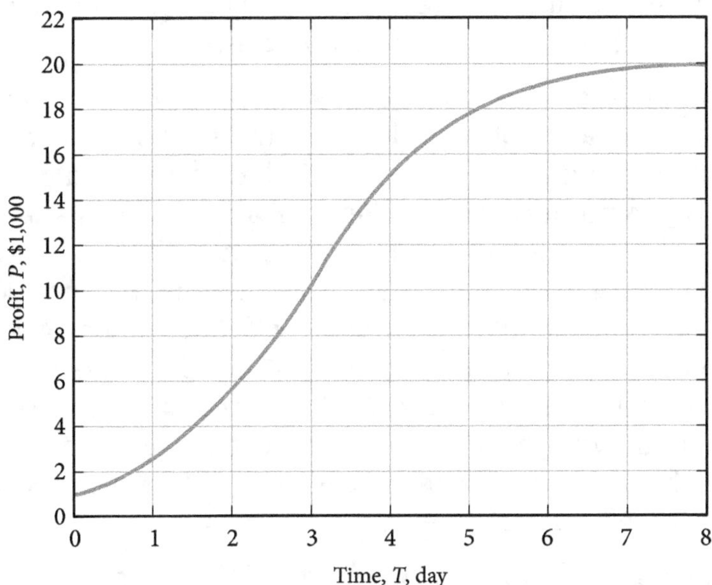

Figure 28. Profit and Time to Design

Table 16. Marginal Profit Increase with Time

Work Period (day)	Increased Profit ($/day)
0–1	1,500
1–2	2,900
2–3	4,600
3–4	4,600
4–5	2,900
5–6	2,000
6–7	600
7–8	200

The small improvements that occur over the latter periods of work can have a profound impact over time. As an example, energy usage in the United States is a complex topic, and the role of engineering can be difficult to tease out. However, it is safe to say that marginally designed engineering improvements in the conversion, transmission, generation, and conservation of energy have been major factors in efficiency gains.

Energy intensity is a measure of how much energy is required to produce each dollar of gross domestic product (GDP), a measure of economic output. In 1990, the United States used 8.7 units of energy to produce each dollar of GDP, but a remarkable fact is that while energy use in the US increased by 26% between 1980 and 2014, GDP increased by 149% during the same period. That represents about a 2% increase of goods and services per year per unit of energy used, over 35 years. This GDP growth is staggeringly beneficial to the country in terms of national security, economic growth, personal wealth, and overall quality of life. The seemingly modest yearly improvement of 2% per year produced significant results over time.

Engineering is said to be as much art as it is science. A joke tells about an engineer who had worked at a plant for many years and then retired. Soon after that retirement, a problem arose at the plant, and the company asked the engineer to return as a consultant to identify the problem. The engineer returned, talked to the technicians, and read a few gauges. It took thirty minutes. The engineer then took a piece of chalk, placed an "X" on a valve, and said that that valve needed to be replaced. The valve was replaced, and the problem was solved. Soon after, the company received a bill for $1,000. The company complained that the bill was too high for half an hour of consulting and asked for an itemized bill. The engineer replied with a cost of $1.00 for the chalk and $999 for knowing where to place the X.

The potential value of knowledge and experience is illustrated in Figure 29.

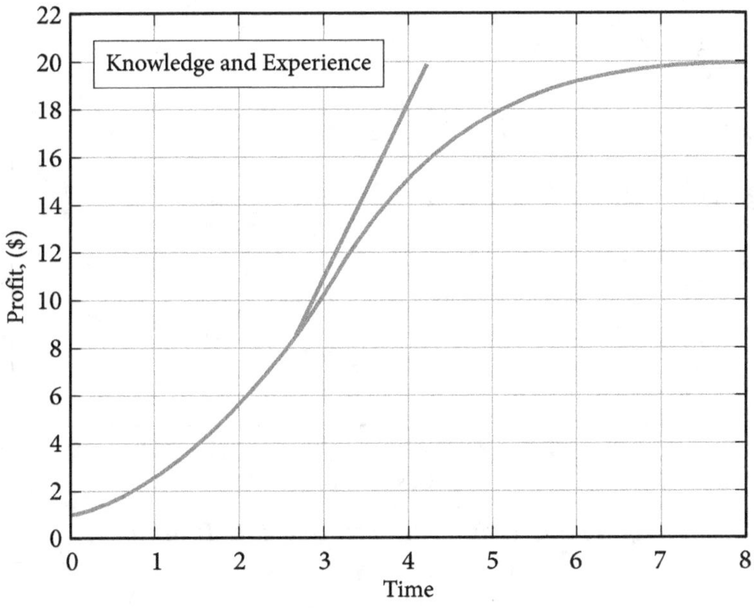

Figure 29. Value of Knowledge and Experience in Design

Another hypothetical example of engineering at the margin is reducing a pollutant in water. Referring to Figure 30, assume that it costs a water treatment plant $100,000 to reduce a pollutant to a level of 0.68 ppm (parts per million). At a cost of $200,000, the pollutant could be reduced to about 0.32 ppm. The next

$100,000 reduces the pollutant to about 0.22 ppm, and so on. Each additional dollar spent to reduce the pollutant is less effective than the prior. Reducing the pollutant to zero is impossible. It must be decided at what point the cost of reducing the pollutant further is no longer desirable. As is the case in much of engineering design work, there are thresholds that must be met. For example, the Environmental Protection Agency has developed drinking water standards under the authority of the Safe Drinking Water Act. However, after meeting the minimum standard, the opportunity cost of each additional dollar spent must be considered.

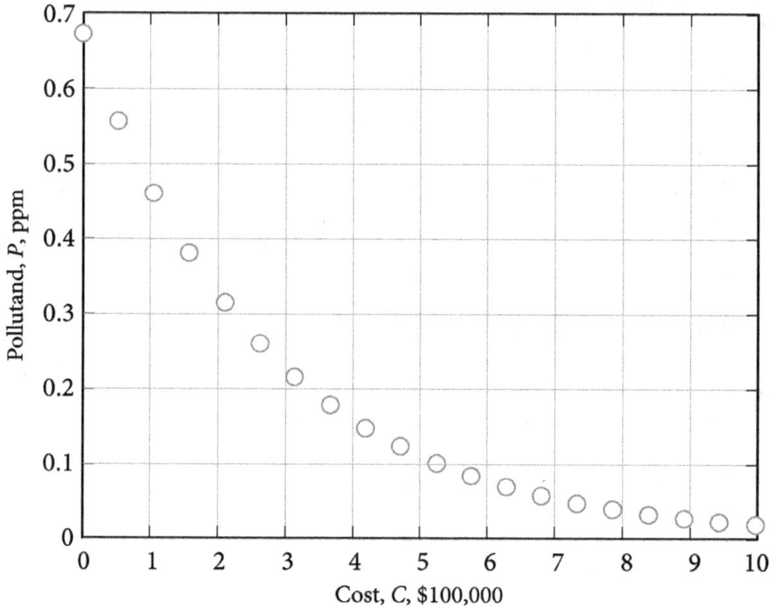

Figure 30. Treatment Cost to Reduce Pollution

3.3 First Principles

A first principle is a foundational theory or assumption from which solutions are developed. They are the bedrock of any design. They can be used unquestioned as they are accepted as fundamental concepts and relationships because they have been proven to be reliably predictive through extensive verification and useful application.

As discussed in the introduction, Newtonian physics is used in most engineering work. It is based on Newton's theory of gravity. Perhaps the most fundamental of his first principles is his second law that states: force equals mass times acceleration ($f = ma$). We use this because it can adequately model most of the problems we solve.

Below are a few examples of first principles and their use in answering engineering questions.

3.3.1 Forces and Moments

Forces are constantly influencing the physical world. They cause objects both to move and to not move. They have both a magnitude—for instance, lbf or N—and a line of action. The arrow, called a vector, indicates direction, and the length of the arrow sometimes represents the magnitude of a force. Recall that force equals mass times acceleration and that weight is a particular type of force where the acceleration is that due to gravity on earth (g), where $g = 9.81$ m/s^2 or 32.2 ft/s^2.

Consider a box with a weight of 750 N. As that box sits on the floor, a weight of 750 N is acting downward (toward the center of mass of the earth). If the box is not moving up or down, the floor must be exerting a force of 750 N straight up. The sum of the vertical forces are equal in magnitude and opposite in direction (see Figure 31). All the forces acting upon the box are of a magnitude and direction that sum to zero if that box is not moving. Other forces include the force created all around the box

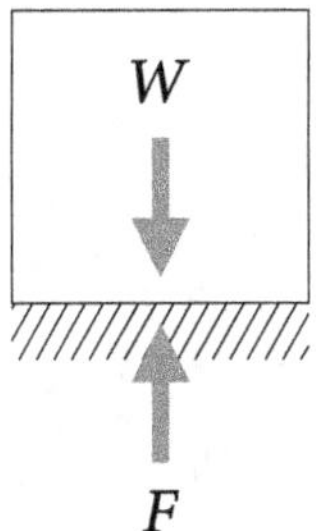

Figure 31. Opposing Forces on a Box

because of atmospheric pressure. Those forces are also equal and opposite. If the sum of all the forces acting on an object were not zero, the object would be moving. Likewise, if a 35.0 lbf object was suspended by a string, the object would create a 35.0 lbf weight in the downward direction and the string would be in tension (tension is a type of force) with a 35.0 lbf force acting upward.

A force acts anywhere along its line of action. For example, in Figure 32, the 25.5 N force acts anywhere along its line of action as shown by the dashed line.

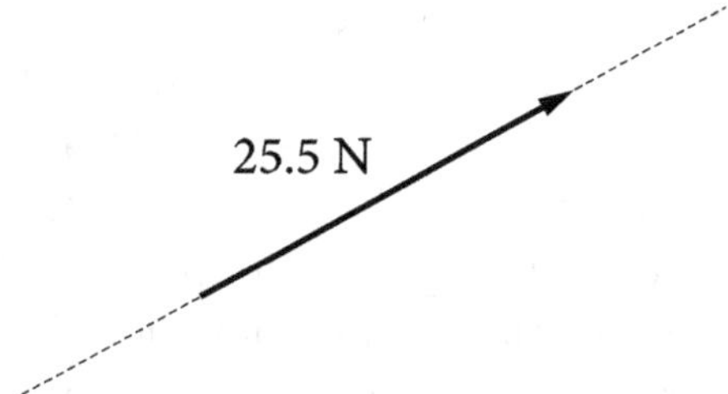

Figure 32. Line of Action of a Force

A pulley translates the line of action of a force as shown in Figure 33. Note that the rope is in tension on both sides of the pully. Consider a weight that is suspended by a pulley and is held stationary by the force (F) downward. That force could be applied anywhere along the rope (thereby creating tension along the rope to keep the weight stationary). If the force were greater or less than the object's weight, the object would move up or down accordingly.

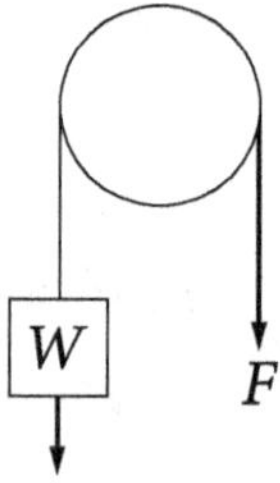

Figure 33. Line of Action with a Pulley

Another characteristic of weight is that a distributed weight can be represented by a single weight acting from the center of gravity (CG) of an object. Consider a meter stick that has a weight distributed along its length (see Figure 34). That distributed weight can be represented by a single weight acting from its center of gravity as shown in Figure 34. To demonstrate this, you could hold up that meter stick with a finger that is placed at its center of gravity, and the finger exerts an upward force that is equal to the weight of the entire stick.

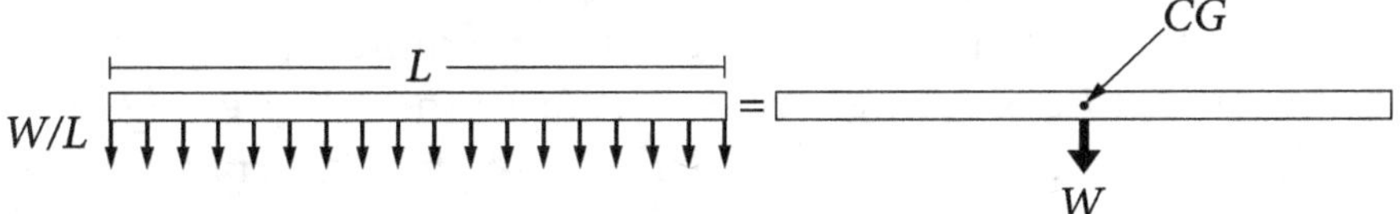

Figure 34. Distributed Force Acting at a Point

A moment (often called torque) is the product of a distance (called a moment arm) and a force, which has units of $[F][L]$ such as ft-lbf or $N - m$. A moment arm is defined as *the perpendicular distance from the line of action of a force to the point in question.*

Consider Figure 35, where a wrench is being used to turn a nut. A force is applied to the wrench, where the length of the wrench is the moment arm. If the nut does not turn as desired, then

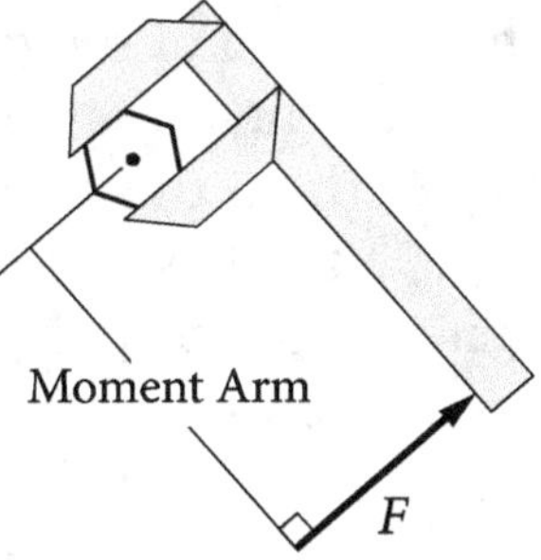

Figure 35. Illustration of Moment Arm

either the moment arm or the force, or both, could be increased, thereby creating a greater moment. If the moment arm were doubled (perhaps by using a length of pipe over the handle), then the applied moment would be doubled. Likewise, doubling the force applied would double the moment. If both the moment arm and the force were doubled, then the applied moment would be quadrupled.

3.3.2 Statics

For an object to be stationary (static), the summation of both the forces and moments acting upon it in in all directions must be equal. For simplicity, we will work in two dimensions only. By convention, forces acting downward or to the left are negative, and forces acting upward or to the right are positive. Traditionally, moments in a clockwise direction are considered negative, and counterclockwise moments are considered positive.

Consider the seesaw shown in Figure 36. For the seesaw to remain stationary, the product of $(W_a)(D_1)$ must equal the product of $(W_c)(D_2)$. If the products are not equal, the seesaw will rotate because of the unbalanced moment. For example, if $W_A = 30$ lbf, $D_1 = 5.0$ ft, $W_C = 10$ lbf, and $D_2 = 15$ ft, the moments are balanced, and no rotation would occur. The *point* about which we are taking the moments in this case is point B, which is a hinge. Moments are often taken about a hinge because the sum of the moments must equal zero if the object is static. In this example, we ignored that the sum of the forces must equal zero, but we used two negative weights. If an object is static, the sum of the forces must equal zero. In this case, there is an upward force of 40 lbf at the hinge, but it has a moment arm of zero with respect to the hinge. Thus, the complete equation to calculate the moments about point B is $+(30$ lbf$)(5.0$ ft$) + (40$ lbf$)(0.0$ ft$) - (10$ lbf$)(15$ ft$) = 0$. Note that the positive and negative signs refer to the direction of the moment, not the force. For example, the 30 lbf is in the negative direction, but the force creates a counterclockwise moment, so the moment is positive.

Recall that an object is static when the sum of moments acting upon it are zero; otherwise, it would be rotating. Using the seesaw again as an example, assume that the coordinate at point A is $(0, 0)$.

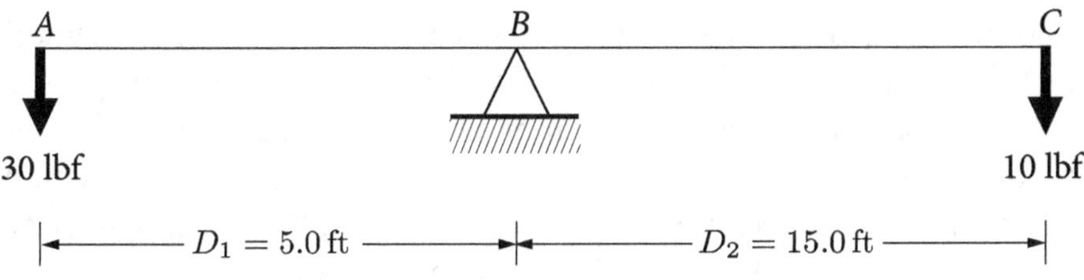

Figure 36. Moment Illustration

What is the sum of moments about the arbitrary point $(30, 20)$?

$$+(30 \text{ lbf})(30 \text{ ft}) - (40 \text{ lbf})4(25 \text{ ft}) + (10 \text{ lbf})(10 \text{ ft}) = 0$$

You may want to review the math, and especially the signs of the moment, to ensure that you understand.

3.3.3 Archimedes' Principle

> *Any object, wholly or partially immersed in a stationary fluid, is buoyed up by a force equal to the weight of the fluid displaced by the object.*

> Archimedes

Well over 2,000 years ago, Archimedes determined the concept of buoyancy and its relationship to an object's geometry and weight. The power of this principle is its simplicity and utility. Realizing and quantifying this phenomenon is one of the best examples of understanding physical relationships. It doesn't require sophisticated math or specialized education, only an interpretation of words and knowledge of weight and volume.

As a reminder, the specific weight (γ) of a material or substance is its weight divided by its volume. For instance, the specific weight of water is 62.4 lbf/ft^3, which is equal to 9.81 kN/m^3. The density (ρ) of a material or substance is its mass divided by its volume. For instance, the density of water is 1.94 slug/ft^3, which is equal to 1,000 kg/m^3.

The specific gravity of a material or substance is its density divided by the density of water or its specific weight divided by the specific weight of water. It is a unitless dimension. If the specific gravity of an object is greater than 1, it will sink in water, and if the specific weight is less than 1, it will float. For instance, the specific gravity of concrete varies quite a bit, but is about 3 and concrete will therefore sink, while the specific gravity of polypropylene plastic is about 0.9 and this substance will float.

Example 1.

Imagine that a cylindrical log is floating half-submerged on a pond. The weight of the log is acting downward, and the buoyancy force caused by the displacement of water is acting upward at an equal magnitude. The volume of the displaced water is equal to half the total volume of the log (the portion submerged). Because the specific weight of water is $62.4 \frac{\text{lbf}}{\text{ft}^3}$, the specific weight of the log must be $31.2 \frac{\text{lbf}}{\text{ft}^3}$.

To demonstrate this, assume that the volume of displaced water is 23.0 ft^3. This is also the volume of the submerged portion of the log.

Weight of the log:

$$(\text{Volume of the displaced water})(\gamma_{\text{water}})$$

$$= (23.0 \text{ ft}^3)\left(62.4 \frac{\text{lbf}}{\text{ft}^3}\right) = 1,435 \text{ lbf}$$

Example 2.

A cube of concrete with 1.000 m sides and a density of $2,400 \frac{\text{kg}}{\text{m}^3}$ is fully submerged at the bottom of a pond. The density of water is $1,000 \frac{\text{kg}}{\text{m}^3}$.

What is the weight of the submerged concrete?

The elevation at the bottom of the pond is 0.0 m. The elevation of the water surface is 5.0 m. as the concrete block is raised from elevation 0.0 m to elevation 7.0 m. All block elevations refer to its bottom surface.

Weight of the unsubmerged concrete:

$$(\text{Volume of concrete})(\rho_{\text{concret}})(g)$$

$$= (1.000 \text{ m}^3)\left(2,400 \frac{\text{kg}}{\text{m}^3}\right)\left(9.81 \frac{\text{m}}{\text{s}^2}\right) = 23,500 \text{ N-down}$$

Force of buoyancy on the fully submerged concrete:

$$(\text{Volume of displaced water})(\rho_w)(g)$$

$$= (1.000 \text{ m}^3)\left(1,000 \frac{\text{kg}}{\text{m}^3}\right)\left(9.81 \frac{\text{m}}{\text{s}^2}\right) = 9,810 \text{ N-up}$$

Net weight of submerged concrete $= 23,500 \text{ N} - 9,810 \text{ N} = 13,690 \text{ N-down}$

Figure 37 shows the solution

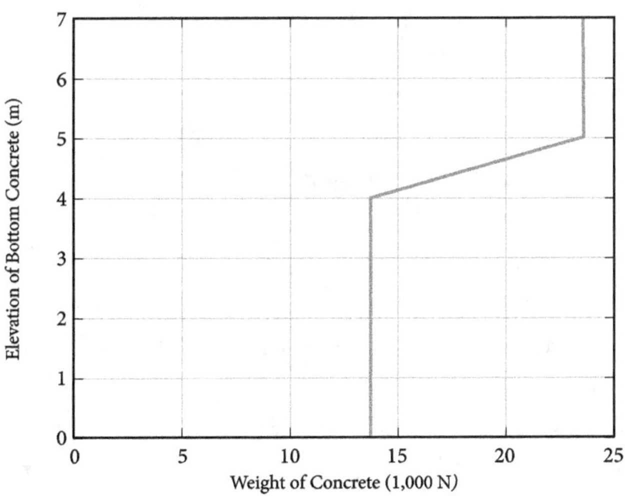

Figure 37. Weight of Concrete Cube in Water

Example 3.

Referring to Figure 38: a wooden sphere with a radius of 1.00 ft is attached to the bottom of a pool of water with a rope. The sphere is entirely submerged. If the specific gravity of the wood is 0.75, what is the tension on the rope?

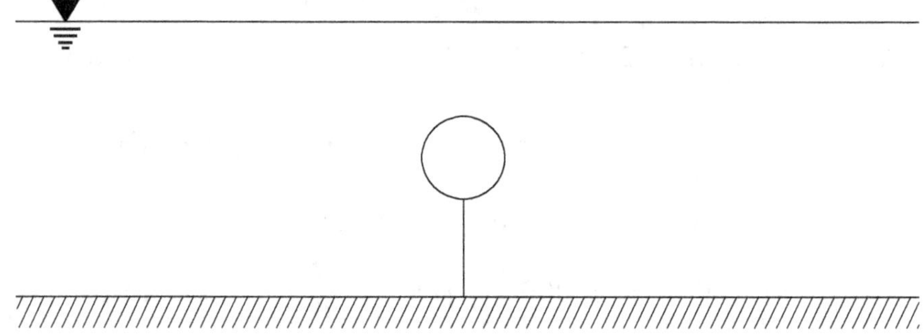

Figure 38. Submerged Wooden Sphere

Volume of sphere is

$$\frac{4}{3}\pi r^3 = \frac{4}{3}\pi(1.00)^3 = 4.19 \text{ ft}^3$$

Weight of displaced water

$$= 62.4\frac{\text{lbf}}{\text{ft}^3}4.19\,\text{ft}^3 = 261 \text{ lbf}$$

Weight of sphere

$$= (0.75)\left(62.4\frac{\text{lbf}}{\text{ft}^3}\right)(4.19\,\text{ft}^3) = 196 \text{ lbf}$$

The difference between the force of buoyancy and the weight of the sphere is 65 lbf, which is the tension in the rope.

3.3.4 Bernoulli's Equation, revisited

Bernoulli's principle (also known as the energy equation) is used in the context of the energy associated with flowing fluids, as we saw in section 2.3.3. The energy in a fluid is constant with respect to velocity, pressure, and height. These are referred to as velocity head, pressure head, and elevation head, which can be written as:

$$\frac{v^2}{2g} + \frac{p}{\gamma} + Z = \text{constant} \qquad (3.1)$$

We can add these energy forms because they all have units of length. Work through the units to convince yourself that this is true. It is common to compare the energy in a fluid between two points. If the fluid has velocity, then losses (largely because of friction) between the two points need to be taken into consideration:

$$\frac{v_1^2}{2g} + \frac{p_1}{\gamma} + Z_1 - \text{Loss} = \frac{v_2^2}{2g} + \frac{p_2}{\gamma} + Z_2$$

Example 4.

Referring to Figure 39, determine the difference in pressure from the top to the bottom of an open-topped tank of oil $\left(\gamma_{\text{oil}} = 8.83 \frac{kN}{m^3} \right)$ filled to a depth of 3.00 m. The oil has no velocity, so both velocity heads and losses are zero. Assume the elevation at the bottom of the tank is zero, and for convenience, the atmospheric pressure is considered to be zero. Point 1 is at the oil's surface, and point 2 is at the bottom of the barrel.

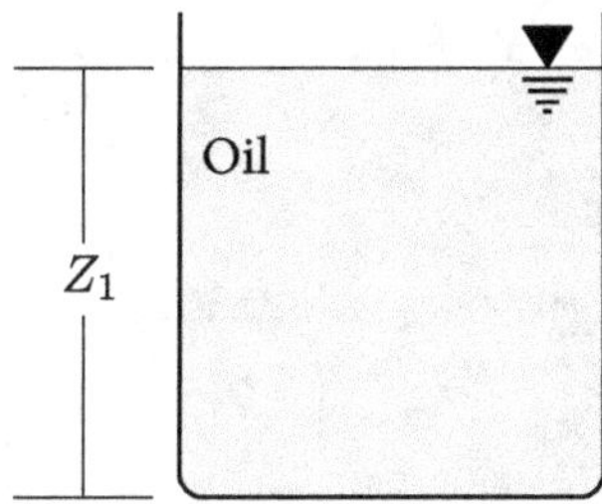

Figure 39. Pressure Differential in Open-Topped Tank of Oil

Bernoulli's equation simplifies to: $Z_1 = \dfrac{p_2}{\gamma}$

$$3.00 \text{ m} = \frac{p_2}{8.83\dfrac{\text{kN}}{\text{m}^3}}$$

$$p_2 = 26.5\frac{\text{kN}}{\text{m}^2}$$

Example 5.

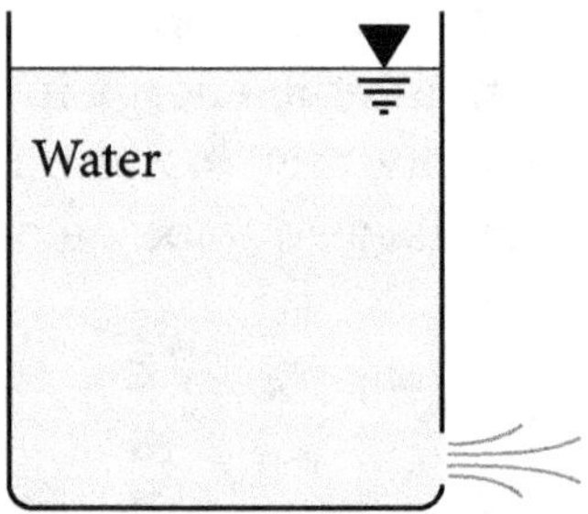

Figure 40. Water Flow from Open-Topped Tank

Water flows from an orifice at the bottom of an open-topped tank (Figure 40). What is the velocity of the exiting water when the depth of water is 2.00 ft? Ignore losses. Point 1 is at the water's surface where the atmospheric pressure is assumed to be zero. Point 2 is at the orifice where the exiting water is also subjected to atmospheric, or zero, pressure. Assume that velocity at the water surface is zero. Find the velocity of the exiting water.

Bernoulli's equation simplifies to: $Z_1 = \dfrac{v_2^2}{2g}$ (known as Torricelli's equation).

$$2.00 \text{ ft} = \frac{v_2^2}{2\left(32.2\dfrac{\text{ft}}{\text{s}^2}\right)}$$

$$v_2 = 11.3\frac{\text{ft}}{\text{s}}$$

Example 6.

The measurement for volume of fluid passing a given point over a period of time (e.g., gallons per minute) is the volumetric flow rate ($[L]^3[T]^{-1}$), often abbreviated as Q. In pipe flow, Q is frequently calculated by multiplying the velocity of the flow times the cross-sectional flow area. Consider water flowing through a constricted pipe at a constant flow rate as shown in Figure 41.

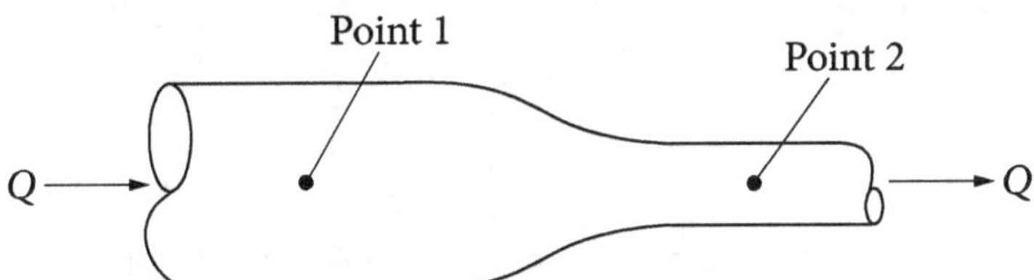

Figure 41. Illustration of Volumetric Flow Rate

The pipe diameter at point 1 is 12.0 in, and the pipe diameter at point 2 is 6.00 in. As a result, there is a greater flow area at point 1 than point 2. Therefore, because the flowrate is constant, the water's velocity at point 1 is less than its velocity at point 2.

Situation and assumptions:
- Points 1 and 2 are at the same elevation.
- Q equals $5.00\ \dfrac{\text{ft}^3}{\text{s}}$.
- Assume a pressure of zero at point 1. This can be assumed because the problem is to find the *difference* in pressure.
- $\gamma_{\text{water}} = 62.4\dfrac{\text{lbf}}{\text{ft}^3}$

Applying Bernoulli's equation for flow between points 1 and 2, determine the pressure difference between the two points.

$$\text{Diameter } 1 = 12.0 \text{ in}, \quad \text{Area } 1 = \pi(0.500 \text{ ft})^2 = 0.785 \text{ ft}^2$$

$$\text{Diameter } 2 = 6.00 \text{ in}, \quad \text{Area } 2 = \pi(0.250 \text{ ft})^2 = 0.196 \text{ ft}^2$$

$$\text{Velocity 1} = \frac{Q}{A_1} = \frac{5.00\frac{ft^3}{s}}{0.785\ ft^2} = 6.37\frac{ft}{s}$$

$$\text{Velocity 2} = \frac{Q}{A_2} = \frac{5.00\frac{ft^3}{s}}{0.196\ ft^2} = 25.5\frac{ft}{s}$$

$$\text{Velocity head 1} = \frac{v_1^2}{2g} = \frac{\left(6.37\frac{ft}{s}\right)^2}{2\left(32.2\frac{ft}{s^2}\right)} = 0.63\ ft$$

$$\text{Velocity head 2} = \frac{v_2^2}{2g} = \frac{\left(25.5\frac{ft}{s}\right)^2}{2\left(32.2\frac{ft}{s^2}\right)} = 10.1\ ft$$

Because we are looking for a pressure difference between the points:

$$\frac{v_1^2}{2g} + \frac{p_1}{\gamma} + Z_1 - \text{Loss} = \frac{v_2^2}{2g} + \frac{p_2}{\gamma} + Z_2$$

$$0.630\ ft + 0 + 0 - 0 = 10.1\ ft + \frac{p_2}{\gamma} + 0$$

$$9.47\ ft = \frac{p_2}{62.4\frac{lbf}{ft^3}}$$

$$p_2 = 591\frac{lbf}{ft^2} = 4.10\frac{lbf}{in^2}\quad \text{less than } p_1$$

Conclusion

> *It [engineering] is a great profession. There is the fascination of watching a figment of the imagination emerge through the aid of science to a plan on paper. Then it moves to realization in stone or metal or energy. Then it brings jobs and homes to men. Then it elevates the standards of living and adds to the comforts of life. That is the engineer's high privilege ... To the engineer falls the job of clothing the bare bones of science with life, comfort, and hope.*

Herbert Hoover, Engineer and President of the United States

Herbert Hoover's quote is the best definition of engineering that I know. (See the text of the entire speech at the end of the chapter.) Practicing engineering arguably gives you the best way to positively impact millions of people around the world. When working under good government, an individual in no other profession can come close to achieving a goal of many good people in this world—the lessening of human suffering.

While, most often, the medical profession comes to mind with respect to improving physical human health, consider here the role of engineering. Many medical breakthroughs today, as a matter of fact, are possible because of the devices produced and analysis performed by biomedical and other engineers.

However, there is a strong argument that the largest factor in health improvement over the last 150 years is the availability of abundant clean water. These achievements are firmly in the realm of engineering.

In the United States, from 1900 to 1936:

- Typhus deaths decreased 96%, with 26% of the reduction attributed to abundant and readily available clean and plentiful water.

- Child mortality decreased 81%, with 61% of the reduction attributed to clean water.

- The total mortality rate decreased 30%, with 43% of that reduction due to clean water.

In the United States today, mortality from waterborne disease is essentially zero, and this is a major factor in life expectancy at birth increasing from 47 years in 1900 to 76 years in 1998.

An excellent example of an individual engineer who greatly improved the lives of countless people is Henry Darcy. In the early nineteenth century, cities grew ever larger, resulting in poor water quality. As detailed above, the available water often carried diseases such as typhoid fever, cholera, and dysentery. Darcy developed an inexpensive method of filtering large quantities of water and delivering that clean water to cities. From his work, Darcy's law and the Darcy–Weisbach equation were both developed, and they continue to be used to this day. Throughout France and elsewhere in Europe, these water sources remain and continue to improve the lives of individuals. Darcy's work represents the essence of engineering by improving the human condition through the knowledge and clever application of scientific principles.

"Darcy's work is also an example of the role of engineers in society. As a profession, society expects that engineers will only work in areas of competency, be objective and truthful, act in the interest of their employer, and conduct themselves ethically. Most importantly, though, is that they "hold paramount the safety, health, and welfare of the public." To my knowledge, engineering is the only profession that is obligated to society above all others. For instance, medical and legal professionals are primarily obligated to an individual patient or client. Darcy's work clearly demonstrates the engineer's obligation to serve society. All people, regardless of wealth, power, or any defining characteristic, have had access to clean water and all its benefits.

While virtually unknown today, the significance of Darcy's achievements was well understood at the time. He was awarded the Legion of Honor by King Louis Philippe, a gold medal from the city of Dijon, and his final resting place is inscribed, *"He conceived the project, made all the studies, pursued to the end the execution of the works to which Dijon owes the creation and the abundance of its public waters. Doubly benefactor of his native town through his talent and his selflessness."*

Today, engineering is as important as ever. As scientific knowledge advances, so does the possibility to solve increasingly complex problems. The combination of new knowledge and a clever mind can create solutions that were previously unimaginable. Critical to these technological advancements is that society supports education and research. Equally important is that society values the objective truths discovered through this work.

For the individual, I believe the most important characteristic of a successful engineering student or practicing engineer is curiosity. Engineering is hard. Solving complex problems can be tedious, often frustrating, and sometimes fails. Being smart helps, but a high IQ doesn't necessarily predict success. It's not intelligence that keeps a student studying at 2:00 in the morning—it's curiosity. And it is curiosity that motivates the practicing engineer to continue learning and to be willing to fail in pursuit of a new or better solution.

A good example of the willingness to fail while pursuing a better solution is private companies launching spacecraft. In 2010, a private company, SpaceX, launched a craft to orbit and then recovered it. It is difficult to overstate the significance of this. Until then, the only entities able to do this were the governments of a few countries.

Perhaps more impressive is that in 2015, SpaceX recovered the first stage of a rocket, after live broadcasting two failures, with a vertical landing that would allow the first stage to be reused. This is now routine and will decrease the cost of space flight dramatically.

It is often said that we engineers stand on the shoulders of giants. That is certainly the case here, where a private company uses lessons learned from the United States and other countries as they developed space flight over the last five decades.

Today, the desire to make the world better continues uninterrupted from the earliest times of human history. Global warming, disease, poverty, and developing appropriate energy sources are among the most pressing needs for the profession to address.

An additional and often overlooked contribution we can make is to actively engage in politics. Our education, experience, and approach to problems equally valuable in the halls of Congress as they are on the manufacturing floor. We understand the power of the science and the magic of ingenuity. We know the limits of our knowledge and the uncertainty of our decisions. We understand the need to compromise due to conflicting constraints. Most importantly, we agree to work for the common good.

While acknowledging the challenges we face, it is important to remind ourselves of our accomplishments. By almost any objective measure, the human condition has improved dramatically over the recent past. In 1981, 40% of the world lived in extreme poverty— today, it's about 10%. In 1990, 76% of the world's population had access to clean water; in 2015, it was 91%. In 1976, the world's literacy rate was about 69%, and today, it's 86%.

A critical driver of these advancements is increased efficiencies, and increasing efficiency is largely in the domain of engineering. Those innumerable and hard-fought incremental increases in efficiency result in great advancements.

Having the necessities of life produced and delivered more efficiently frees resources such as time, money, and ingenuity. These newly released scarce resources can then be put to work elsewhere such as better education and government. This creates a virtuous cycle of freeing more resources and developing better solutions.

Engineering is a great profession. We have a proud past and a future of limitless possibilities.

Complete text of Herbert Hoover's speech from the beginning of this chapter:

> *It [engineering] is a great profession. There is the fascination of watching a figment of the imagination emerge through the aid of science to a plan on paper. Then it moves to realization in stone or metal or energy. Then it brings jobs and homes to men. Then it elevates the standards of living and adds to the comforts of life. That is the engineer's high privilege.*
>
> *The great liability of the engineer compared to men of other professions is that his works are out in the open where all can see them. His acts, step by step, are in hard substance. He cannot bury his mistakes in the grave like the doctors. He cannot argue them into thin air or blame the judge like the lawyers. He cannot, like the politicians, screen his shortcomings by blaming his opponents and hope the people will forget. The engineer simple cannot deny he did it. If his works do not work, he is damned.*
>
> *On the other hand, unlike the doctor, his is not a life among the weak. Unlike the soldier, destruction is not his purpose. Unlike the lawyer, quarrels are not his daily bread. To the engineer falls the job of clothing the bare bones of science with life, comfort, and hope. No doubt as the years go by, people forget what engineer did it, even if they ever knew. Or some politician puts his name on it. Or they credit it to some promoter who used other people's money. But the engineer himself looks back at the unending stream of goodness which flows from his successes with satisfaction that few professions may know. And the verdict of his fellow professional is all the accolade he wants.*

Herbert Hoover,
Engineer and President of the United States

Bibliography

Appelbaum, Binyamin. "As U.S. Agencies Put More Value on a Life, Businesses Fret." *New York Times*, February 16, 2011.

Hobbes, T. *Leviathan*, 1651.

Hughes, S. W. "Archimedes revisited: a faster, better, cheaper method of accurately measuring the volume of small objects." *Physics Education* 40, no. 5 (September 2005).

Miller, D. C. "The Role of Public Health Improvements in Health Advances: The Twentieth-Century United States." *Demography* 42, no. 1 (2005): 1–22. http://www.jstor.org/stable/1515174.

Nadel, Steven, N. E. *Energy Efficiency in the United States: 35 Years and Counting*. Washington, DC: American Council for an Energy-Efficient Economy, June 2015. www.ourenergypolicy.org/wp-content/uploads/2015/07/e1502.pdf.

National Aeronautics and Space Administration (NASA). *Mars Climate Orbiter Mishap Investigation Board Phase I Report*, November 10, 1999.

National Society of Professional Engineers. *NSPE Code of Ethics for Engineers*. https://www.nspe.org/resources/ethics/ code-ethics.

Siceloff, S. *SpaceX Launches Success with Falcon 9/Dragon Flight*. NASA, 2010.

Simmons, C. T. "Henry Darcy (1803–1858): Immortalised by his scientific legacy." *Hydrogeology Journal* 16 (2008): 1023–1038.

SpaceX. *About SpaceX*. https://www.spacex.com/about.

The World Bank. "World Development Indicators." Last updated October 18, 2018. https://datacatalog.worldbank.org/dataset/world-development-indicators.

Urban, T. *The Elon Musk Blog Series: Wait But Why*. Austin, TX: Lioncrest Publishing, 2016.

U.S. Department of Transportation, National Highway Traffic Safety Administration. "Quick Facts 2016, DOT HS 812 451." Accessed October 2017.

U.S. Energy Information Administration. "Independent Statistics and Analysis." Accessed June 2018. https://www.eia.gov/totalenergy/data/browser/index.php?tbl=T01.01#/?f=A.

U.S. Federal Reserve Bank of St. Louis. "Gross Domestic Poduct (GDP)." Accessed June 2018. https://fred.stlouisfed.org/series/GDP.

U.S. Patent and Trademark Office. "2104 Inventions Patentable—Requirements of 35 U.S.C. 101 [R-08.2017]." Last modified January 24, 2018. https://www.uspto.gov/web/offices/pac/mpep/ s2104.html.

World Bank. "Energy Intensity Level of Primary Energy (MJ/$2011 PPP GDP)." Accessed June 2018. https://data.worldbank.org/indicator/EG.EGY.PRIM.PP.KD.

World Heath Organization. "Key Facts from JMP 2015 Report." http://www.who.int/water_sanitation_health/monitoring/ jmp-2015-key-facts/en/.

Table of Equations

1.	$P = \sin\left(\dfrac{180°}{N}\right)(N)(D)$	Perimeter of a polygon
2.	$\sigma = \sqrt{\dfrac{1}{N-1}\sum_{i=1}^{N}(x_i - \overline{x})^2}$	Standard deviation of a sample
3.	$f(x) = \dfrac{1}{\sqrt{2\pi\sigma^2}}e^{-\frac{(x-\overline{x})^2}{2\sigma^2}}$	Normal curve
4.	$Z = \dfrac{x - \overline{x}}{SD}$	Z-score
5.	$y = mx + b$	Linear function
6.	$y = kx^m$	Power function
7.	$y = ke^{mx}$	Exponential function
8.	$\dfrac{v_1^2}{2g} + \dfrac{p_1}{\gamma} + Z_1 - \text{Loss} = \dfrac{v_2^2}{2g} + \dfrac{p_2}{\gamma} + Z_2$	Bernoulli's Equation between Two Points
9.	$\dfrac{v^2}{2g} + \dfrac{p}{\gamma} + Z = \text{constant}$	Bernoulli's Equation at a Single Point

Table of Figures

Table of Tables

Cover Explanation and Credits

The cover photograph was recently taken in the small village of Lessy, in the Lorraine region of northeast France. The town's population was 400 in the seventeenth century, and today the number is about 850. Prior to the mid-nineteenth century, clean spring water from the Mount St Quentin mountains was captured and transported to the town by way of a series of canals and tunnels to provide water for agriculture and a small flour mill.

With increased travel in the early nineteenth century, cholera spread from Asiatic regions to Europe, reaching France about 1830, at which time Lessy built its first public water fountain. Around 1850, a second cholera pandemic swept Europe, and the current lavoir was constructed and its canals and tunnels improved to bring the filtered spring water to the village. The cause of cholera was unknown, but it was generally believed to be related to "miasma," a foul-smelling odor in the air. Because human waste and level of cleanliness contributed to odor, this theory suggested a nexus between water quality and the disease. In 1854, the eminent English physician John Snow clearly demonstrated water's role in the spread of cholera by mapping outbreaks in the city of London and the locations of water supply. It was, however, decades until the germ theory of disease transmission was established and more efficient methods of improving water quality were developed.

The lavoir in Lessy, like others in countless cities and villages, provided free, clean, and ample water to all citizens. The benefits were immense. It greatly reduced the effort needed to procure water, improved health, and served as the village laundry. Like many others, Lessy's lavoir makes water available at a pipe where it can be collected for household use. The water then flows to a basin where clothing is washed, flowing to a second basin where clothes are rinsed. The ground around the lavoir is paved and roofed to prevent mud from soiling the area. Before the lavoir, clothes would be carried to the river, washed, and then carried back wet and heavy, making laundering long and laborious work. The river water was not clean, the banks were muddy, and winter ice was a challenge. Now, clean household water and laundry facilities were available in the village itself. Perhaps as important as these benefits, the lavoir was, and remains, a gathering place where friendships and communities are made and maintained.

The lavoir was made available to all at no cost until 1954, last used as a laundry in 1973, and provided potable water until the late 1990s, at which time regulatory testing costs became prohibitive. Today, it continues as the village gathering place, and in the summer, children play in the water-filled basins as their parents visit.

Credits:

Mr le Maire Michel Francois. Personal communication.

Rachel Braussen, resident of Lessy from 1978 to 1991. Personal communication.

Jean Marie Reitz, *History of the Lavoir in Lessy*, 2006.

Francine Didelot, Cover photograph.

Acknowledgements

This work would not exist without the encouragement, skills, and kindness of many. The more I thought about those responsible for bringing this book to fruition, the longer the list became. A year ago, I was diagnosed with brain cancer, making me and this book's creation especially dependent upon others.

Virginia Tech's Department of Education generously allowed me to work remotely and between treatments. It fell to my colleagues to teach my classes, continue my committee work, and manage a variety of my other duties. They did so without hesitation and in addition to their own responsibilities. Most importantly, my students received excellent instruction and completed their courses without interruption. The staff submitted paperwork and worked out administrative details. The department cared.

I am particularly grateful to my department head, Professor Jenni Case, for allowing me to continue work on a modified schedule as the diagnosis progressed. My assistant department head, Professor Ken Reid, shouldered most of the burden created by my absence and provided both flexibility and encouragement. While I hope that this book will be valuable to a large audience of advisors, first-year engineering educators, potential engineering students, and beginning engineering students, my primary goal is that it is useful to Virginia Tech's Engineering Education department and students.

Engineering is important, but its methods and accomplishments are largely unknown. I chose to self-publish so this book would be available to a diverse audience at minimal cost. I needed help. I was fortunate to find several talented people that brought this book to completion. Jude Prashaw designed the cover, and Teddi Black further refined it. Jean Hall edited the manuscript while Todd Landsman edited and verified the technical content. Megan McCullough then laid out the document and formatted it for publishing. Tom Adams reviewed the technical content for clarity.

As an engineering student, I studied the contributions of great scientists and engineers such as Manning, Darcy, Bernoulli, and Mulholland in capturing, storing, and supplying water. As a practicing engineer, I had the privilege of working for two of the greatest water development agencies in the world, the U.S. Bureau of Reclamation and the U.S. Army Corps of Engineers. This background led to my fascination with the lavoirs and fountains of France. My friends in the village of Lessy allowed me to explore and understand the details of their lavoir. Michel and Marie Francois welcomed my family and me as their own and tirelessly sought answers to innumerable questions. As mayor, Michel gave me his time and knowledge to visit and explain the tunnels, sources, and canals of the lavoir. My dear friend Rachel Braussen was an indefatigable source of information and, with my abysmal knowledge of the language, an essential translator. Madam Francine Didelot graciously allowed me to use her photograph of Lessy's lavoir.

The University of Vermont medical school is well-known for their expertise in cancer treatment, and I had no doubt that I was in competent hands. What I did not know was the kindness of their care. Overseeing my treatment is Dr. Alissa Thomas, with Dr. Christopher Anker and Dr. Philip Kiely contributing their expertise. Equally important are the administrative staff, technicians, and nurses who keep track of my health, schedule appointments, smooth out the hiccups, and apply my treatments. Everyone involved in my care has been nothing but kind.

Finally, I thank my family. My sister Cathy has patiently endured hours of my complaining and replied with understanding and encouragement. My son Alec, whose writing ability far exceeds my own, was instrumental in the shaping and editing both the introduction and conclusion.

I don't have the words—and if I did, I would not have the space—to acknowledge all that my ex-wife, Jude Prashaw, has done, and continues to do. I know the degree of her love. I only hope that I can adequately express the depth of my gratitude.

Ottawa, Ontario, Canada
19 October 2018

Jeffrey Connor taught engineering at Virginia Tech for twenty years. His interest and experience in the field began after high school when he worked as a technician in land surveying and navigation at sea. After earning his graduate degree in civil engineering, he put his experience and education to work on a variety of federal water projects and received his professional engineering license.

www.ingramcontent.com/pod-product-compliance
Lightning Source LLC
Chambersburg PA
CBHW061505250726

48657CB00005B/1727